THE BUSINESS OF YOGA

How to Start and Grow Your Yoga Business

Art Tiddens
e-mail: art-proteus@cox.net

© <u>The Business of Yoga</u> Astraea Corp. 2002 . All rights reserved. No part of this publication may be reproduced, transmitted, transcribed, or translated into any language, in any form, or by any means, electronic or mechanical, including photocopying, recording, or by any information storage and retrieval system without the written permission of Art Tiddens and Astraea Corp..

For information, contact Astraea Corp., 6332 Via Real, Carpinteria, Ca. 93013. Ph. 805-566-9409, Fax 805-566-9509.

Disclaimer: Please Read This!

I have done my very best to provide you with useful information throughout this manual, but I can not and will not guarantee that the information is correct or necessarily applicable to your particular business or situation.

Laws, procedures, regulations, tax codes, etc. change frequently, vary by jurisdiction, and are subject to different interpretations.   It is your responsibility to verify all information, all laws, all forms, and all procedures discussed in this manual before relying on them.

Throughout this manual, there are numerous reminders to get professional help. <u>Nothing in this manual can substitute for timely and qualified legal or accounting advice</u>. In all situations involving local, state, or federal law, obtain specific information from the appropriate government agency or a competent professional.

INTRODUCTION

The Business of Yoga

This book is for the yoga teacher who knows all about yoga and about teaching, but may be less knowledgeable about business and how to organize, run, and grow the business end of teaching yoga. The book's origin goes back three years to a conversation I had with Ana Forrest. At that time, she invited me to develop a business course to be taught during her three week Forrest Yoga Teacher Training courses (which were being offered several times a year around the country). Her concern was that teacher training courses such as hers put new yoga teachers out into the community well-trained in all things yogic, but unable to open a business checking account or write a business plan. Her own experiences mastering business skills added a personal element to her request. An eight-hour business course and a 200-page companion manual grew out of that original conversation. Since then, the business course manual has been revised several times, adding and deleting material as experience and student feedback dictated. This most recent revision is designed to be a stand-alone text.

After three years of teaching "The Business of Yoga," several common themes kept reappearing. First, many of the students think of business with fear, or boredom, or disdain. Others feel that yoga should be above business and that mixing the two can only be to yoga's detriment. Second, while there are all kinds of business resources available, online, on book shelves, and elsewhere, much of the material is complex and intimidating to the new yoga teacher who just wants some basic business information specific to his or her business needs. There is almost no material out there that is directed specifically to the yoga teacher. I hope this book offers a remedy to both of these problems.

The Business of Yoga is a primer for the yoga teacher who wants to learn or improve on the basic business skills of running a business. My goal has been to make the book fun and easy to read yet informative — you can not learn the lesson if it puts you to sleep. In the text you will find stories and anecdotes, along with lots of lists and forms that will help you get going. Throughout the text there are checklist questions, which are reprinted together at the end of the book. There are workshop questions at the end of each section so you can practice what you have learned.

The book is divided into four sections: planning your business; starting your business; running your business, and growing your business. The majority of the book addresses the business issues of what I call the solo yoga teacher. That is a teacher who works for himself or herself as an independent contractor — teaching at one or more studios, and perhaps teaching private classes as well. The later section of the book addresses many issues related to opening your own studio and running that type of business. However, I'll inject a word of caution about this up front. Along with the popularity of yoga has come an overabundance of yoga studios. We can all observe this. In the small town where I live, where there was once one studio there are now five or six. Can they all make it? Or will there be a consolidation as the growth and popularity of yoga slows?

While I feel that this is the best, most specific and basic book for the solo yoga teacher, it is by no means the only book you should read. Whatever your interest and experience, there are many other good books and resources. Many of them are referenced throughout the text as well as listed in the appendix. One general business book that anyone considering starting a business should read is Paul Hawken's Growing a Business.

While you are undoubtedly passionate about yoga, I suspect you have mixed feelings about business. I hope to change that. I want to expand and explode your notions of business, and broaden and deepen your business knowledge. More than that, I think I can make the process fun and very informative. Most of all, I can save you time and a lot of aggravation by helping you with the tools of business.

I believe the whole notion of business is largely misunderstood, particularly in the holistic/green community, and I will say first that I am an advocate of good and honest businesses. And they are everywhere. The media would have us believe that all business is corrupt big business, cigar-chomping fat cats who feed off their unsuspecting shareholders and use company accounts as their personal and very large piggy banks. It's good copy, and in the case of Enron and Tyco just happens to be true. But as is often the case, this is a very small part of the whole picture.

This country was built and continues to prosper and innovate, on the strength of small businesses. From the pre-revolutionary bakers, coopers, and farmers to today's hi-tech start-ups, entrepreneurship is a tradition in this country. In fact today, about half of our country's economic output (the GDP) is generated by small businesses.

There is no question that entrepreneurship has brought the bad with the good, particularly in our material and increasingly polluted world. But if we are to remedy those problems, the solutions just might come from right-minded businesses that offer "green" products and solutions, or yoga studios that offer a different way of being in the world. These are businesses too.

All businesses, good or bad, run on the same machinery--the same basics. Whether it's General Electric or your small yoga business, both have sales, clients, expenses, and budgets, pay taxes, and have plans for the future. Large or small, in any business it is essential to become proficient at using all the business tools that are available.

Whether we are aware of it or not and whether we like it or not, we are in business every day. Many of our interactions with other people are transactions or negotiations. We learn from a young age to be salesmen, to market ourselves, to lobby for what we want or need. (Whether we are good or bad at it and what dysfunctions we pick up along the way are other issues.)

Small businesses arise for a variety of reasons, but they are all acts of creation, and can be as creative and imaginative as their owners. You may go into business because of a great idea, or to make a product or provide a service that you cannot find, or because you just have to be involved in something you love. The good news is that if you decide to start a business it can be the most liberating, creative process imaginable. Of course that is the bad news as well — *it is all up to you*! *Small businesses are as good or as bad as their owners' efforts and attitudes.*

Think of what you like to do, where you like to be, what you like to eat. More than likely there is some small business involved, one that is changing and evolving everyday. *Business is above all a creative and dynamic process*.

If you remember nothing else from this book, please take this with you.

<u>In a small business, your business is you, and you are your business</u>. Bring what you stand for and what you value to your business. Remember its products, services, and employees all represent you. The business will grow and evolve, but your values should be in place from the beginning. The Golden Rule applies here too. (Basically, treat others as you would like to be treated.) The very things we strive for as humans, compassion, honesty, and integrity are prerequisites in a right-minded business. They are the right thing to do. And your business will be the better for them.

Art Tiddens

Table of Contents

	Page
Preface	1
Introduction & Welcome	3
Table of Contents	5
Course Description & Objective	7
About your Instructor	8
The Big Picture (Course Outline)	10
Part I – Planning Your Business	
Let's Talk Business	11
Ten Reasons to Go into Business	13
Short Stories on Business	15
Truths & Myths about Money	20
Business Ethics	22
Some Thoughts on Business	24
The Business Plan	28
The Essential Parts of a Business Plan	30
Checklist for the Business Plan	35
Sample Business Plans	36
Part I Workshop	60
Part II – Starting Your Business	
Getting Going	63
Business Cards & Resumes	65
Approaching a Business	68
Insurance	76
Licenses, Permits, Paperwork	81
Pricing, What Should I Charge?	85
Marketing	86
10 Keys to Successful Marketing	99
Part II Workshop	100

Table of Contents (cont.)

Part III-Running Your Business	
What is Bookkeeping?	103
What you Need to Get Going	104
Simple Ledgers	106
Simple Bookkeeping Terminology	107
Computers, Spreadsheets, vs. Ledgers	119
Sole Proprietorships & Tax Prep.	125
Part III Workshop	132
Part IV-Growing Your Business	
Growing Your Business	136
Getting a Roof Over Your Business	138
Debts, Loans & Leasing	147
Other Business Structures	149
Employees, Leadership & B. Relations	151
Six Steps to Improve your Business	154
Putting It All Together	160
Business Checklist	161
Part IV Workshop	163
Appendix	
Nine Key Concepts to Remember	165
Exit Survey	167
Book & Resource Guide	169

About the Manual

This manual will help students develop the basics of starting and growing a successful yoga business or small business. The manual contains: specific and detailed information on basic business issues; two sample business plans and a business plan checklist; sample bookkeeping ledgers and spreadsheets; basic tax forms and how to use them; examples of necessary business and license forms; marketing ideas and examples; a step-by-step guide for starting a yoga business; a self-diagnostic checklist for existing businesses, and a reference section for written and online resources.

About the Author

Art Tiddens heads Astraea Corporation, a small-business and investment-advisory firm, founded in 1989, and located in Carpinteria, California. The firm evaluates all aspects of businesses and investments for clients. Art holds a doctoral degree from the University of California, Santa Barbara and his Ph. D. dissertation, *Aquaculture in America: The Role of Science, Government, and the Entrepreneur*, was published by Westview Press. He holds a Bachelor's degree in biology and a Masters degree in biochemistry. Art has also done post-graduate work at a joint program sponsored by Stanford and the London Business School. He is currently at work on another book about business and investing.

"Make everything as simple as possible, but not simpler. " - Albert Einstein

THE BIG PICTURE

This manual is divided into four parts.

PART I   **PLANNING YOUR BUSINESS**
- Business Issues
- Money Issues
- Business Ethics
- Creating a Business Plan
- Sample Business Plans

PART II   **STARTING YOUR BUSINESS**
- Business Cards & Resumes
- Interviews
- Insurance, Licenses & Paperwork
- Pricing
- Marketing

PART III **RUNNING YOUR BUSINESS**
- Bookkeeping
- Ledgers
- Accounting Terms
- Bookkeeping & Computers
- Sole Proprietorships & Tax Prep

PART IV   **GROWING YOUR BUSINESS**
- Adapting, Growing
- Leasing Space
- Debts &Loans
- Other Business Structures
- Business Relationships
- Steps to Improve & Grow Your Business
- Business Checklist

PART I

1.) Let's Talk Business. What is Business? What am I in for?

("Being in business is not about making money. It is a way to become who you are."
–Paul Hawken)

Business means many things to many people. The term comes from Middle English "to be busy," which is exactly how many people would describe their nine-to-five jobs. It sounds pejorative, and for many it is.   Most of us would describe business as some kind of entity formed to make money by charging for a product or service. For many people, "business" means big business, both terms being synonymous with greed, corruption, and all that is wrong with our country and capitalism. Without question, there is a lot of "baggage" and bad feelings about business.

"I hate my job!" "I'm just doing it to make some money, so I can do what I really love." "That business is just out for a quick buck, and will screw everybody they can." "This whole economy is just about money and profit." These are all valid expressions of what we hate about business.

But I would suggest that for every bad business out there (the corrupt ones, the dishonest ones, the ones without passion or compassion), there are an equal number of good businesses. These are the businesses (whether non-profit or for profit) that provide valuable services and products, as well as inspired leadership in their industries. That's what we're after, and small businesses can fit nicely into this ideal.

This country was founded on the idea of personal freedoms. And the ability to work for yourself (as opposed to working for the landed gentry in England) was and is an important part of those freedoms.   Small business (largely agriculture) dominated colonial life. Today, small businesses still continue to be an important part of our economy. The small business share of private sector gross domestic product is about 50%. Considering the billions of dollars in revenues for companies like General Electric, this is an amazing number. More importantly, small businesses can be a dynamic source of innovation. They can also be a source and a voice for right-mindedness and constructive change.

Small businesses come alive for many reasons. Who among us hasn't had dreams of writing a book, teaching, or opening a small yoga-clothing store?   Most of us dream of these businesses not because we were all business majors in college and can't wait to "go into business." Rather, we daydream because we are passionate about an idea and want to share it with others. Most people don't start their small businesses with the idea of getting fabulously wealthy. And to think that success is only measured by money is missing the bigger picture. Your business will reward you and challenge you in ways you never dreamed of. It will make you think, allow you to play, force you to grow and innovate. It will demand much of you. If you think that opening your own business is an easy way out, a way to beat the system, or just a way to make money --- well, you're in for a shock.

Most small business owners work extraordinarily hard to establish themselves, protect and expand their 'niche' in their industry, and, if they are tenacious and lucky, build a brand name and franchise. (A franchise in this sense is a recognized name – with pricing authority. That is, customers will pay up for the name because its product or service is worth more to them than a competitor's.)

People go into business for a variety of reasons, although there do seem to be a couple of common denominators. Often, it is recognizing that there is a need for a particular service or product, something that entrepreneur needs and cannot find. (The organic and natural food business began this way.) Sometimes it is out of necessity. (I'm out of work, maybe I'll start washing and detailing cars.) Hopefully, it is always out of a passion for what you are about to do.

Working for yourself and running a business requires self-honesty, self-awareness, a desire to change and grow, and the ability to respond to events that you may or may not have any control over. **Much like your yoga practice, in your own business there is no place to hide.** For me, and maybe for you, this is the good news. But for many people, this type of job is simply not for them. It is easier to go to a nine to five job where tasks are well-defined and put in front of you, where there is a regular paycheck and benefits, where the job ends at 5:00 pm and you can occupy your thoughts, efforts, and free-time elsewhere. Working for yourself, and running a small business can be heaven, but it can also be hell. Before you take any other steps toward starting a small business (and that includes quitting your job to start teaching yoga), you need to decide if such a move is the right decision for you.

Taking the time, at the beginning, to have an honest conversation with yourself is the most important step you will ever take in creating your business. "Know thy self" is the old saw. But here it is especially true, and better now, than later.

Many successful small businesses begin simply and easily--they just seem to happen. An after-work interest turns into a part-time job, and later grows into a business. Perhaps in your case, practicing yoga becomes a passion, lands you in teacher training, and soon thereafter you are teaching a couple of classes a week at your local yoga center. However, your dream can be quickly ruined if it is transformed from something you love into a business you hate.

You may love practicing all day long. Maybe you can't get enough of various teacher-trainings and weekend workshops. And it may seem a natural transition to teaching as the next logical step; or opening a yoga center, or a yoga clothing store, or even a health food bar next to your favorite yoga studio. But each one of these requires different skills, has very different rewards and risks, and puts very different demands on you than when you were simply practicing yoga every day. Remember that there is a world of difference between taking a yoga class after work to relax, and being mentally and physically prepared to teach five classes each day to pay the rent.

Try to learn what you are about. What do you honestly like and dislike about the business you are considering? (And don't, for one minute, think you can ignore or delegate the things you don't like--they will always end up right back in your lap.)

Small businesses are successful not just because the owner can make his own living. In the best circumstances the owner is able to shape his life and work around his interests. He is passionate about what he does and brings authenticity and integrity to it. These traits shine through. If you are the customer, client, or student of such a business, you'll notice it immediately. The line of work matters not at all. A waitress can bring these traits to her job--and you notice. I have been in yoga classes where the teacher could not be less interested in being there—and it was obvious. **Professionals, people that approach what they do with passion, integrity and intention, are noticed and appreciated, and more often than not those values and enthusiasm are reciprocated.**

So before you build a business plan, give up your day job, or rent studio space, think long and hard about what you are getting into. Ask yourself:

Is going into business for myself something I want to do and can do?

Am I passionate about the business I am considering?

The Business of Yoga

2.) Ten Reasons To Go Into Business. Ten Reasons Not To.

("The difference between 'involvement' and 'commitment' is like an eggs and ham breakfast: the chicken was 'involved'-the pig was 'committed.")

Ten Reasons To Go Into Business

1.) You love what you do; it's not work.
2.) You have an idea you want to share with the world.
3.) You want to determine your own destiny, and don't mind working hard to get there.
4.) You want to be challenged, to grow, to learn, and to innovate.
5.) You are not afraid to change your view of what business can be.
6.) You want to change the world.
7.) Your idea or activity is an essential part of who you are.
8.) You enjoy the creative act and want to create something new.
9.) You're not afraid to make mistakes and learn by them.
10.) You want to inform, transform, improve and delight your customers, clients or students.

Ten Reasons Not To Go Into Business For Yourself

1.) You're searching for an identity.
2.) You have a lot of money, but need something to do.
3.) You don't want to work with others.
4.) You don't know what else to do.
5.) You want to change the world.
6.) You don't want to work hard.
7.) You have an MBA degree.
8.) You don't want to take problems home with you at the end of the day.
9.) You want to be a boss, the one in charge.
10.) Working for others puts too many demands on you and your time.

Before you start a business, ask yourself:

Why do I want to go into business? What am I going into business for?

3.) Short Stories on Business with a Few Quick Lessons

("Experience is a hard teacher because she gives the test first, the lesson afterwards."- Vernon Sanders Law)

The depth and width of businesses is almost limitless. But whether the business is in service, sales, or manufacturing, all businesses must have the permission of the marketplace--the permission of customers and clients-- to succeed. Finding what works, what brings customers and clients to you, is a crucial and dynamic process. The small business owner has to be able to think through what his business is about, and learn and innovate as he goes along.

In each business below there is a lesson to be learned about starting and surviving as a small business.

<u>Zephyr Carpet Cleaning</u> A friend of mine started his small carpet cleaning business after he grew tired of bartending and waiting tables. After majoring in art in college, starting his own business seemed like a good way to find employment. He quickly hired a couple of young strong guys, lined up clients, and was off and running in the "rug sucking" business. He did well for a while, but kept losing employees — nobody enjoys cleaning carpets for long. He particularly disliked sucking rugs, and it was physically hard on his body and back. He eventually gave up the business. **The lesson: Make sure you enjoy and can do the core part of your business. More often then not, any element of your small business can (and often will) end up in your lap.**

<u>Pacific West Water</u>   Another friend runs a water business in northern California. He has more pure "tradeskill" than anyone I know. He has a natural ability to find businesses that make money. Initially, Pacific West was selling solar panels for heating water. This was a good business until our government removed large tax incentives on the purchase of solar equipment. Then the bottom fell out of the solar panel business. So Barry moved into the big purified water machines that you see in front of groceries stores. That worked for a while, and then a few big companies took over that market. Pacific West responded by moving into small water purification systems for the home and office. In each case, as market conditions changed, Barry took his knowledge and expertise and adapted. **The lesson: In any business you have to adapt to the many factors that affect your business.**

<u>Hawaii Jack</u> My other friend with tradeskill is a photographer, former Navy Seal, and avid surfer who moved to Hawaii for the surf. After assorted jobs, he noticed that no one in Hawaii had the lock on certain services that were controlled by big companies on the mainland. These services simply did not generate enough business for the bigger companies to establish a presence in the islands. Today, Jack has a collection of small

service businesses-- everything from erecting stadium seating for small sporting events to coin lockers on Waikiki Beach. These businesses allow him to surf and support his family. **The lesson: Keep an eye out for overlooked niches.**

A Word on Tradeskill:
In my mind this is a somewhat nebulous but effective set of skills that allow people to start and run a business. The authors of *Honest Business* (Michael Phillips and Salli Rasberry) believe there are four such skills: persistence, the ability to face facts, knowing how to minimize risks, and being a hands-on learner. To these, I would add a fifth: knowledge of and an intuition for the marketplace.

Stir Crazy Coffee   About two years ago, the small town I live in got our very own Starbucks. While I have mixed feelings about the company, they seem to do things well and are certainly a force to be reckoned with. And they are always busy. Recently, a small coffee shop, Stir Crazy Coffee, opened three doors down from Starbucks. It's too early to predict how they will do, and in one way I'm cheering for them. But it seems as if they'll be swimming upstream all the time, and competing on price and against a brand name without any significant difference in their service or product. Crazy might be an appropriate name. (After I wrote this, I saw a Wall Street Journal article that noted just the opposite effect. Apparently, there is a synergistic effect around some of the Starbuck locations, and competitors can survive on the overflow — still?) **The lesson: Choose your battles carefully; a niche might be better than head to head competition.**

Jet Blue   I can't say any aspect of this airline qualifies as a small business, but the lesson here is a good one for any business. Here's a business that is going head to head with big established brand names and grabbing market share. By revamping the airline business model, they are competing with and beating the established airlines. Their secret is cost efficiencies generated by a simpler business model. Where United and the other big airlines have all kinds of different planes (that require different pilots, mechanics, and handlers), Jet Blue flies one type of plane. Where the others have a variety of fares that are confusing and require time, money, and effort to quote fares and issue tickets, Jet Blue has a simple fare structure. **The lesson: Think different. Think Simple. There is always room for innovations or new ideas in any business, even old established ones.**

Microsoft   Microsoft started as a small business and might have remained one except for an early, gutsy, and insightful move Bill Gates made when Microsoft was small and had little going for it. In the early 1980s personal computers were new and not yet in the mainstream of American life. IBM was developing its personal computer, which would jump-start the whole industry. The IBM team developing the PC went looking for a software operating system for it, stopping first at a company in Monterey, Ca., that had developed a popular software product called CPM. The CEO and owner was out, flying his plane, and someone suggested Microsoft so the IBM "suits" went up to Seattle and met with Gates. They explained what they were doing and asked Gates if his company had a software product that could fit their needs. Gates said they did, and got IBM to agree to use his product exclusively. Gates, in fact, had nothing approaching what IBM needed, but knew where to look. He found what he needed at another company in Seattle and bought it for around $50,000 dollars. A clause in the sales agreement allowed Microsoft to re-sell the software. That operating system and derivatives of it are in over 90% of the world's personal computers, and among other things made Gates the world's richest man. **The lesson: When opportunity knocks be ready and be creative. A little luck doesn't hurt either**.

The last two stories help to illustrate the difference between a commodity business and a franchise or branded business. In the former business you compete on price, in the latter on name, reputation, and service.

Aquaculture   For many years I was involved in the business of aquatic husbandry (growing plants and animals in a water habitat), as a scientist, farmer, and analyst. Aquaculture is just farming in water; boy, is it like farming. I would define a commodity business as one that competes on price. Farming is a good example. When avocados, potatoes, or any crop is in short supply (due to disease, weather, etc.), supply goes down and price goes up. Often the price attracts new growers and soon everyone is planting the crop and the price plummets. The same thing has happened in salmon aquaculture. As soon as the process for rearing pen-farmed salmon became standardized, production took off and the price has fallen. **Lesson: In a commodity business, you always compete on price, and supply and demand. These become the major drivers of your business.**

Surfboards   Yet another friend has a thirty-year old business making and selling surfboards. From the very beginning he has worked hard to build a reputation as a top-notch board designer and shaper. Over the years he has built excellent brand name recognition, and surfers are willing to pay more for his boards. His company does not compete on price or volume — it doesn't have to. The old saw goes, "no amount of money will replace a good name or a good reputation. "   This is largely true. The New York Times is The New York Times.   Starbucks has become Starbucks. Both stand for something. Both would be hard to compete against or duplicate. **Lesson: Try to build** a brand name and a reputation from the start. Separate yourself from the pack. Unless you're a Costco and it's planned, try not to compete solely on price.

A final thought on brand names and reputation. Think about the difference between a yoga studio that simply rents space, hires a bunch of teachers and hangs out a sign, versus one that has a strong leader/teacher and over time builds a reputation for its particular method of yoga, outstanding teaching, and a dynamic, authentic program. I would submit that one is competing with the local YMCA, and every other athletic firm or studio in town that offers yoga. The other is competing with itself.

Business is a type of economic Darwinism. The marketplace and your customers or clients will give you permission to be in business or withhold it. Restaurants that serve over-priced, bad food don't last. Beginning yoga teachers that charge $1,000 an hour won't find students. The corner gas station that charges a lot more than his neighboring gas stations won't get much business. The corner store that is not clean and has obnoxious help will not get customers. **Think like your customers. What will bring customers through the door and keep them excited and interested?**

As you are planning your business ask yourself:

What can I learn from other businesses as I start and grow my own business?

BUSINESS LESSONS

Get interested in how other businesses do things. Read, look, listen, and learn as much as you can from other business stories.

It is said that experience is the best teacher. While that is true, I would add that learning from the experiences of others is cheaper and less painful.

Here is a summary of the business lessons from above.

- Make sure you enjoy and can do the core part of your business. At some point, all elements of your business will end up in your lap.

- In business, you always have to adapt and change.

- Keep an eye out for overlooked niches.

- Tradeskill is: persistence, the ability to face facts, minimizing risks, being a hands-on learner, and having a knowledge and intuition for the marketplace.

- Choose your battles. A niche is often better than head-to-head competition.

- There is always room for innovation in business, even old established ones.

- When opportunity knocks, be ready; be creative.

- In a commodity business, you always compete on price. Consider building a franchise business.

- Business is a type of economic Darwinism.

- Think like your customers. What excites them? What gets them in the door? What brings them back?

4.) Truths & Myths about Money. A Different Way to Look at Money.

("No profits grow where no pleasure is taken." – William Shakespeare, *The Taming of the Shrew*)

By the time we're old enough to think or worry about money, it often carries some kind of charge with it. Few people are neutral on the subject. We hear: "Money is the root of all evil," "I'm only in it for the money," "Money can't buy happiness," and all sorts of other comments about money. Sometimes it is suggested that the purity or message of yoga is somehow lessened if money is involved. Somehow, yoga should be a gift to your community. Maybe the practice of yoga belongs to everyone and no one should profit (or profit too much) from it.   Implied in all of this is the idea that somehow money ruins things.

I would suggest that ethical and right-minded pursuits can co-exist alongside money, and that profit is not necessarily a bad thing. In fact, I suspect that all the negative baggage associated with money belongs elsewhere--within each of us. For some people, many of their emotions are wrapped up and hung up on money. John Steinbeck wrote that humans are caught "in their lives, in their thoughts, in their hungers and ambitions, in their avarice and cruelty, and in their kindness and generosity too—in a net of good and evil." We often use money to pacify or exacerbate these feelings. Fear and greed, our identity, sometimes our sense of self-worth can all be wrapped up with money. Yet as hard as it is to detach money from many things, **I suspect that money is not evil, it's neutral. What we put on money is largely our own issues.**

There is no question that we need money to survive. And for those that think yoga should be a gift to the community or somehow bartered, I would suggest that money is really the middleman for barter. If we lived in some small village in Tibet, it might work out that teaching a yoga class could really be your gift to the community. And your students, who might be your landlord, baker, and butcher, could return the favor in gifts or barter. For better or worse, our society is quite a bit more complicated. But money might be viewed as a simple medium to untangle an endless series of trades between you and your work, your landlord, the grocery store, the auto-repair guy, the phone company, and so on.

(If you really want to worry about money, think about what it stands for. It is largely built on faith.   It is based on the strength of our government and economy, and more importantly, on a tacit agreement among all of us that it is inherently worth something. Imagine what would happen if people no longer accepted currency. What if the guy at the Speedy-Mart said, "No I won't take those dollars for the gas and Twinkies? I need gold or two chickens.")

The point of all this is to have another conversation with yourself about money. Get straight on where you are with it. Does a part of you feel guilty charging money for something you love to do? Does another part give it away, or squander it to make up for the guilt? Do you identify so much with money and things that too much will never be enough? Are there childhood issues with money that you keep tripping over?

If you are going to teach yoga or open a small business for yourself, it is important to put money in its rightful place. You are more likely to succeed if you love what you do. But it helps to be clear on money, deal with money issues in a rational and healthy way, and not let old baggage undermine your hard work. It will do little good to buy personal finance books, watch Suzie Orman, or excel at spreadsheets and business bookkeeping if you have unresolved or unrecognized issues about money.

There are three excellent books on this whole money issue and I would recommend all of them. They are: *Honest Business* by Michael Phillips and Salli Rasberry, *The Seven Laws of Money* by Michael Phillips, and *Your Money or Your Life* by Joe Dominguez and Vicki Robin. These books are not so much about personal finance and budgets (we'll discuss those in a later section). Rather, they take on this whole issue of how we view money and how it is viewed in our society, and suggest some alternative views.

Ask yourself:

What money issues do I carry with me?

What were my family's attitudes towards money and wealth?

What are mine?

If I could change one thing about my relationship with money, what would it be?

How might my attitudes towards money help me or hurt me as a business person?

5.) Business Ethics (It's Not an Oxymoron)

("Being a good human being is good business." –Paul Hawken)

Being a good human being <u>is</u> good business, for many reasons. For one thing, you have to live with yourself. By this I don't mean being scared of eternal damnation. I mean, when all is said and done, the company you keep is you. And the best company is someone with integrity, authenticity, and purpose. I am personally mystified at the corporate "wrong-doers" (can't the White House come up with a better name?) that the media is fascinated with. Where's the joy, the sense of accomplishment, and the sense of community, in ripping off your company, its shareholders, and the public? **Good people shine through in business, as in life.** We've all seen them, and they can be waitresses or surgeons, teachers or auto mechanics. Certainly they don't all act the same or behave in a rigidly defined way. But they all have the common traits we keep talking about integrity, authenticity, and purpose.

Your business needs to embrace these traits as well. If you are simply, "Ashley Walker – Yoga Instructor," this is easily accomplished. However, as your business grows and takes on employees, sub-contractors, or consultants, things change. Any aspect and every aspect of your small business represents you, and reflects on you. As a private yoga instructor, if you show up at a client's home late and filthy--that obviously reflects on you. But is it much different if you run a yoga studio and have teachers that do the same thing, or an accountant that forgets to submit forms to the IRS, or a carpenter that does a poor job on your studio floor? **It has been said that, "You are the business and the business is you"---and it is true.**

I believe that you have a competitive edge if you run your business honestly and ethically. While you might benefit in the short run by overcharging, or getting away with less service, or even over-billing, eventually people notice. Right-minded businesses work because customers (by and large) want to be treated well and don't mind paying a fair price. Customers (and students) are smarter then we think, particularly when they get interested in a service or product and, as a result, learn a lot about it. Running a right-minded business does not mean that you shouldn'tt be a tough negotiator nor charge what you think is fair. It does mean that you need to communicate in a clear and honest manner what you are doing and why, and what you are charging and the justification for it.

Honest, well-run businesses that take the time and effort to educate themselves and their customers are usually rewarded.

A good exercise is to be your own customer. How would you like to be treated? Or taught? Or charged? What aspects of your business excite you? What aspects don't? Can you respect your business and how it deals with people? (I hope so!)

What's missing that you as a customer would like to see? (Mints on the Yoga mats? An organic food and juice bar next to your studio?) Don't be afraid to think differently, using who you are and what you stand for to improve and change your business. Authenticity is not about conforming, but being who you are and taking what you are excited about to the marketplace.

Finally, take the time to think about and put in writing your own Statement of Ethics for your teaching and for your business. Keep it available as a source of inspiration. Put it in your business plan, as your ethics or mission statement and make sure the rest of the business plan works with it.

Ask yourself:

Can I bring integrity, authenticity, and purpose to my business?
What are my ethics that I bring to my teaching and to my business?

6.) Some Thoughts on Business Attitudes, Learning, and Information.

("Be the hero of your own life.")

Everyone has his or her own style, beliefs, and way of doing things. I certainly want to encourage that. But there are a few things that may be helpful to keep in mind, as you start your own business.

Much of the discussion and many of the books about business repeat the same old sayings about how to act, what to wear, and what professional etiquette to be aware of. It all reminds me of the plethora of self-help books, personal finance books, and exercise videos. None of the material seems particularly new, and we all know it to some degree, yet the books and videos are always on the best-seller lists. I think it's because we don't act on this material---and we know it.

Everyone knows that at "work" you need to dress appropriately, be dependable, be discreet, and not get drunk at the office party, yet people still do just the opposite. Some of the ideas below seem redundant or obvious, and we're all sick of hearing about them — but that does not mean they are not helpful.

Periodically, *Investor's Business Daily* newspaper runs a feature that lists (what they believe are) the traits of successful people. These include:

How you think is everything.
Be positive. Think success. Don't accept a negative environment.
Set up your dreams and goals and make a plan to get them.
Take action.
Never stop learning.
Be persistent.
Learn to analyze details.
Focus your time and money.
Be different (think different).
Deal and communicate with people effectively.
Be honest. Be dependable. Take responsibility.

To these I would add:

Figure out who you are.
Love what you do.
Be terrific at whatever you choose to do.
Feel lucky, even when you are not.
Be generous in all things, especially spirit.
Think before you act or speak.
Present yourself and your business with integrity, purpose, focus and authenticity.
Be authentic even when others are not.
Be clean and on time, look good, be present, up, and don't drag your stuff into work or class with you.

These are both short lists and the ideas in them are certainly not original. I hope they are helpful anyway. As was said above, there is a lot of material out there on business and business thought. The *One-Minute Manager*, *Who Moved My Cheese*, *The Discipline of Market Leaders*, and *The Eighty/Twenty Principle*, are just a few of the books that have been on the best-seller lists. Does it seem to you that there is way too much information out there? It sure does to me. In fact, there is even a book to help you with ***that***-- *Information Anxiety*.

There *is* too much information out there, and it has become an industry in and of itself. You will find that most of these books and Fortune or The Wall Street Journal, or other business publications are of little use to you. Don't waste your time or money. Instead, I would suggest watching and learning from others in your field and in other small businesses as a better and cheaper way to go.

I think people confuse information with knowledge, and knowledge with wisdom. Information is useless without the other two.

Listen to what David McCullough, a Pulitzer Prize winning author, has to say on the subject.

"Information has become an industry, a commodity to be packaged, promoted and marketed incessantly. The tools for 'accessing' data grow ever more wondrous and ubiquitous and essential if we're to keep in step, we've come to believe. All hail the Web, the Internet, the Information Highway. We're being sold the idea that information is learning, and we're being sold a bill of goods. Information isn't learning. It isn't common sense necessarily. It isn't kindness. Or trustworthiness. Or good judgment. Or imagination. Or a sense of humor. Or courage. It doesn't tell us right from wrong."

As you get into business, there will be all kinds of opportunities in the form of seminars, workshops, books, videos, in fact, everything imaginable that will promise to give you valuable information that can ensure your success. Be skeptical and be cost conscious. **Gain the knowledge, earn the wisdom, but be careful about collecting information and mistaking it for the other two**.

One thing you should pay attention to is your intuition, and signs or signals that keep pointing you one way or the other.

Years ago, my wife and I tried to purchase some land up on a coastal mountain. The parcel had incredible views of the ocean and for a long time we could see nothing else. Obstacles kept getting thrown at us, which we ignored or tried to overcome. The area water company was bankrupt, the road association was under-funded, the property was called "Rattlesnake Alley, and only a small portion of the property could be built on (most of the property was unstable). The list seemed endless. Eventually we listened. I don't think it was a case of not being tenacious (this went on for over a year), and I don't think we were giving up on a dream. In truth, I think we averted a nightmare.

Another lesson along the same lines comes from a passage in *A Voyage for Madmen*, an account of the first single-handed, around-the-world, sailing race. One of the participants (Bernard Moitessier) was sailing his yacht Joshua in the southern ocean near the tip of Cape Horn.

"The west wind was freshening and Joshua was sailing fast, passing south of Stewart Island. Moitessier's dinner was growing cold …because he wanted to pass the longitude of South Trap, a dangerous outlying reef below Stewart Island, before relaxing his vigilance and eating and sleeping. South Trap would mark his entrance to the Pacific Ocean, the last rocky obstacle between him and Cape Horn. He hopped up and down between deck and cabin, listening to and watching the sea, tweaking sheets for speed, rolling cigarettes below. *Joshua* sped along, steered as always by her vane gear (a wind steering device).

In the afternoon dark clouds obscured the horizon to the north, where he might have seen Stewart Island, and a large school of porpoises, perhaps a hundred of them, appeared around the boat, whistling and clicking, turning the water white with their breaching and splashing. Usually, these "playful" creatures swim alongside a yacht, criss-crossing singly or in synchronized groups in front of the bow wave. But that afternoon they gave Moitsessier a show he had never seen before.

A tight line of twenty-five porpoises swam abreast off his starboard side, rushing from stern to bow, and then veering off sharply, always to the right. Again and again and again, more than ten times, they regrouped and made this same maneuver, while the rest of the school behaved in a manner Moitessier construed as nervous: they moved erratically, they beat their tails on the surface, they created pandemonium around the fast sailing *Joshua*. All the while, a single platoon continued its streaking, abrupt right-hand–turn maneuver. To the right. To the right. Moitessier watched astounded.

Finally, instinctively, he looked at the compass, something he had not done in a while with the wind vane doing the steering. The west wind had shifted into the south without his noticing it, and *Joshua* was racing north, not east, towards the reefs of South Trap. Normally, a shift in wind will alter the wave patterns on the surface, and very soon have them running at an angle to the older swell, a visible alteration of the sea state, and immediately felt by a sailor aboard a boat. But that afternoon there was, unusually, little or no swell, and Moitessier, not for the first time in his wreck-strewn life, had been fooled. He altered course to starboard, to the east — to the right, the direction of the porpoise's abrupt turn.

Their behavior changed immediately. Their nervousness, their disruption of the sea surface, disappeared. Now they swam in their usual playful way. And as Moitessier watched them wondering but not wondering at all about what had happened, one large black-and-white porpoise leapt clear of the water and somersaulted twice in the air before flopping back onto the surface. Twice more it leapt out of the sea to perform its ecstatic double somersault. The school remained alongside *Joshua* for another three hours, for a total of five hours, an extraordinary length of time for such a visit. At dusk, when he was well past South Trap, the porpoises disappeared."

The lesson here is obvious, and what a great story.

As you plan and run your business ask yourself:

What attitudes am I bringing into my business?
What information am I listening to? Is it noise or signal?

7.) The Business Plan

(Well begun is better than quickly finished!)

Most new businesses fail from a lack of planning, not a lack of money. Business planning is essential to your success. With small businesses this does not mean that you need to spend a lot of money or hire consultants to plan for every detail. It does mean that you need to think through everything. Keep it simple. Boil your plan down to essentials, and boil it down again. If you don't have a computer, write down your plan on a pad of paper. By creating a plan and writing it down, you will see the whole plan in front of you — see where the holes are, see what you have forgotten. Most importantly, once you have a plan it will change almost immediately-- as you see changes and revisions that need to be made.

Keep in mind that a business plan should take you from where you are starting, to where you want to end up, and remember that those two points are always changing. The starting point can be an idea for a new business, or a business that is two, or ten, or twenty years old. You will want to revise or create a new business plan at various points in your business's life.

Don't be afraid to make mistakes and try lots of different things as you draft your business plan. Mistakes and trial and error are an inevitable part of life. We know this as kids but tend to forget it as adults. Mistakes are also a part of business. The essential point is to fix them and learn from them, both in the business plan and later on in your business.

A business plan is often called the blueprint to your business, and that's OK, particularly if you are lining up money or investors. But in my mind, a business plan should be a bit more dynamic than a blueprint, and you should not be afraid to mess with the lines. You will need a plan and you will need a direction, but you should not be afraid to make changes and adjustments as they become obvious.

While there is no rigid formula for what must be in a business plan, there are a couple of things to keep in mind, as well as a few essentials that every business plan should contain.

Always keep the end in mind, and think and plan for a top-notch business in all aspects, just don't spend that way at first. (More on this later.) No detail is too small to think about, though it may not end up in the plan. Always do things right from the start; most times it is worth the money to do so. (This might mean getting accounting help early in your business, to set up the books correctly. It does not mean that the day you decide to go into business, you should go out and lease a company BMW.)

Know the difference between a hobby and a real business. Without a plan and close attention to the numbers, a business can be out of business in a hurry. (And if *you* don't know the difference, the IRS will tell you. If you don't show a profit for at least three out of five consecutive years, the IRS can call your business a hobby and disallow any losses. This requirement is always being revised, so be sure to check the current Tax Code. Better yet, hire an accountant.) Try and build a "Plan A and Plan B" scenario into your business plan, especially in any financial projections.

A business plan can be as simple as an idea on a cocktail napkin or go on for hundreds of pages. Whatever it is, it should be as simple as it can be, but not simpler. It should be a good blueprint of what it is you are trying to do and where this new business will go, knowing all the while it is not written in stone. When people are writing business plans that involve raising money from a bank or partners, the plans go into great detail. While it is unlikely that you will be borrowing money from a bank, or trying to raise millions of dollars through an IPO, it is a good exercise to use similar formats for your business. Everything you can possibly think about that may involve or touch your business should be considered. Items can always be thrown out later, but they have to be in there in the first place to be evaluated. Once the business plan is written down, you can see the holes and the needed additions and edits.

The essential parts of a business plan are outlined below. But keep a few general ideas with you as you write the plan. If you can, try to start building a franchise from the very beginning. This means that you won't compete on price, but on reputation, on name, on standing for a certain way of doing things. You don't have to know exactly where you are going, but know what you stand for. Don't duplicate; be original; and be authentic.

For our purposes here (starting a yoga teaching career or a small business), your business plans will be more personal and informal than those of the Wall Street variety. Again, the essential ingredient in any business plan is not the form or the length. Rather it is laying out what you are attempting to do, how you will do it, and why it should succeed.

8.) The Essential Parts of any Business Plan include:

The Business Plan Summary or Executive Summary

In many business plans this is called the Executive Summary. I hate the term. I guess it's for busy executive honchos who are so busy and so smart they can get everything they need in a paragraph or two. Anyway, the idea is to summarize, in a few sentences or a few paragraphs, your plan and how you intent to execute it. This is a great exercise in that it forces you to describe the essence of your business. Does the plan make sense once it is distilled down? When all the bells and whistles and emotion and hype are removed, what does it look like? **The Executive Summary should be written last and should be no longer than a page (for our purposes probably a paragraph).**

In the following two examples describing a solo yoga teacher's business, one summary is well thought out and informative, while the other really does not tell us much.

Summary 1 - I love yoga, and want to turn that passion into a career teaching yoga. I also love and want to help older people. My plan is to try and teach in the retirement communities of my hometown. I will form "Ashley Walker – Yoga Instructor" with these goals in mind.

Summary 2 – After practicing yoga for seven years, successfully completing two well-regarded teacher-training programs, and filling in as a teacher at my local yoga studio for the past two years, I am ready to start my own yoga business, "Ashley Walker-Yoga Instructor." Though there are many yoga instructors and a yoga studio in my town, no one is teaching the large number of senior citizens that reside there. I plan to build my business teaching and helping this overlooked group. I have several group contracts and private sessions already in place during evenings and the weekends. I plan to build on these bases and be teaching yoga as a full time profession within the year.

You get the idea. The first comes off as a wish-- the second as a plan. Many business plans are put together specifically to raise money in hopes of funding the business in question. While this may not apply to you, it is a great measure of your business plan. Would friends, investors, or a bank loan you money on the basis of what you've written? Some courses on business plans require you to present the business plan to a bank as the final project. (Incidentally, your local community college and adult education programs might be a valuable resource for you.)

The Business of Yoga

The same thing applies for the sections below. Think realistically and specifically. Remember some of the small business lessons from above. Stir Crazy Coffee comes to mind. Do you really want to open a studio next to a well established studio? (If so, and there may be valid reasons, explain why.)

The Company Description

This section is used to describe your company and the nature of your business. Even if you are a solo yoga teacher, this is an important exercise. Yes, you teach yoga, but what else is your business about? In addition, this is the place to include a mission statement (stating your company's purpose), a values statement (beliefs and principles that guide you), and your goals and objectives for the company. All these force you to describe what makes your business unique – and that is important.

Mission statements are worth further discussion. A good mission statement tells you a lot about a company. In a few sentences it can describe what the company does, what it stands for, and what it believes in. More and more, customers want to know these things about the companies they support. It is no accident that you see mission statements prominently displayed at many places of business.
Below are some examples of mission statements.

Forrest Yoga – "Ana Forrest has spent 30 years developing Forrest Yoga specifically to address Our People's stresses and challenges, both physical and emotional. We use intense pose sequences, compassionately taught, to develop skills in awakening each of the senses. Forrest Yoga teaches you to bring aliveness, using breath, into every cell of your body. This ignites your passion for living. The pillars of Forrest Yoga are *Breath, Strength, Integrity* and *Spirit*. The mission of Forrest Yoga is to create in each of us a sense of freedom, a connection to our Spirit and the courage to walk as our spirit dictates; thus, doing our part in "Mending the Hoop of the People". Forrest Yoga teaches you to Go Deeper, finding your Truth. Then, you take these gifts you have earned Beyond the Mat into the rest of your life."

Garden Way Yoga - "The Mission of Garden Way Yoga Center is to give the student, whether a beginner or advanced student, a place to practice Anusara yoga. It is our intention to keep the teaching of Anusara as close to the way we have been taught as possible. It is incumbent for the teacher to always act responsibly and with the student's interest in mind. No matter what we learn or from whom, we learn the real and only teacher is within."

My Cat, Bonzer - "More Fish! No Dogs!"

Starbucks Coffee – "To establish Starbucks as the premier purveyor of the finest coffee in the world while maintaining our uncompromising principles as we grow. The following six guiding principles will help us measure the appropriateness of our decisions: provide a great work environment and treat each other with respect and dignity, embrace diversity as an essential component in the way we do business, apply the highest standards of excellence to the purchasing, roasting and fresh delivery of our coffee, develop enthusiastically satisfied customers all of the time, contribute positively to our communities and our environment, recognize that profitability is essential to our future success."

Callaway Golf - "Callaway Golf Company is driven to be a world class organization that designs, develops, makes, and **delivers demonstrably superior and pleasingly different golf products** that incorporate breakthrough technologies, backs those products with noticeably superior customer service, and generates a return to our shareholders in excess of the cost of capital."

Often, the values, and goals and beliefs of a company show up in the company's mission statement. They can also be elaborated elsewhere, but they ought to be thought about, refined and written down. How does your company conduct business? How do you relate to your customers, employees, and community?

For example, say right up front, that you and your company believes that good ethics is good business. Or that the company must make a profit to succeed, but that it will also commit to give something back to the community (maybe in trade or volunteer work.)

Company Products or Service

What is your company offering?
What is unique about your services?
What are the benefits to your potential customer?
What makes you different from the other guy?

A good trick is to look at your offerings from the perspective of your students. What do you want them to see? What makes your services or teachings unique so that they will want to come back to you, instead of your competitors?

Market Analysis (The Business Environment)

This section is where you will want to do some research. You need to get to know your market. Who are your potential clients? Where do you find them? How do you get to them to do business with you? This section should also include research on pricing and competition.

Here is your chance to honestly look at what you might be up against. Is there a glut of yoga teachers and yoga centers in your town? Or is the local yoga center always looking for teachers? Are you offering something so different that competition is not really competition — once people understand what you have to offer? Gaining this research and knowledge is easier than you may think. The local Chamber of Commerce, the local paper, or alternative paper, health food store bulletin boards all may have listings of yoga studios and instructors. Leg work, phone calls, and local contacts are another cheap and effective way to find out who is doing what, and who is charging what. Also, once you go back into your community as a teacher instead of a student, and begin teaching and filling in for other teachers around town, you will be on the business end of things instead of the client/student side. Substitute teaching at the various studios around town, talking to other teachers and studio owners will give you a wealth of information.

The Strategic Plan

In this section, you will want to describe how your business is set up and how it will operate going forward. Where is it starting from? Where is it going? Describe your goals and objectives, and the milestones you will use to measure results. Where do you expect it to be in one year? Two years? Five years? Here is where you can flesh out, in fair detail, all elements of the proposed business. The length and detail will depend on how complex the business is. You will want to discuss such things as: how and where the business will operate, how you will tap into your customer base, how you will market and advertise goods and services, what prices you will charge and the justification for them.

Key Personnel & Background

Even if you are the only employee, this section is an important exercise to look at your qualifications with respect to the business. If you don't have one, this can be a starting point for building a resume. (There's more about putting together a resume in a later section.)

Business Risks & Uncertainties

These are often obvious, but again it is a good exercise to write them down. That way, they will serve as a constant reminder vis-à-vis what you are taking on. Again, the more detailed the better. What haven't you considered?

Often, people forget that they will be giving up their jobs, and the steady income and benefits that go with it. This, obviously, is a huge risk. And with the new business there may be no net income for a substantial period. Other concerns might be: is the building you're leasing space in up for sale? Is a new yoga center about to open down the block? What if you are injured and can't teach? Do you live in a town where a teacher-training program is turning out more and more teachers every month?

Financial Projections, Capital Requirements

This section is often guesswork, especially with bigger, more complicated start-ups. And generally, the farther the financial projections go out, the more questionable they become. Often, business plans include a break-even analysis, a chart or spreadsheet that shows at what point in time the business will break even--that is, income will match expenses. While these are a bit of guesswork as well, they will give you an idea of what it will take to get going. Even with a simple business such as Ashley Walker Yoga, it helps to put down projected income and expenses, what amount of capital (money, savings) is available to the business and what kind of large expenses there might be to get the business going. For example, if you start teaching a lot of yoga classes after work, will your old car need new tires or a tune up? Will you find yourself eating out more often, buying new clothes for yourself and equipment for the private classes? Will you need a cell phone? A computer? Business cards? Don't forget health insurance if you are leaving a job that had provided that for you in the past. And remember, even when you get to the break-even point of the business, you are still not covering personal expenses.

You will find on the pages that follow an itemized lists of questions to help you create your own business plan. A simple business plan for a solo yoga teacher follows that. Following that is a detailed business plan for a large yoga studio and boutique. After examining these, you can work on creating your own business plan.

As you plan your business, ask yourself:

Do I have a Business Plan? Is it well thought-out and written down? Do I have a reasonable grasp of what expenses and income will be?

9.) An Itemized Checklist for Creating Your Own Business Plan:

Business Summary
- Write summary last
- Summarize essence of plan
- Read summary. Does it make sense? Can it work?

Company Description & Services
- What is the new/existing business?
- Where is it going? (Point to point)
- What services or products does the company provide?
- What is its mission statement/values?
- What are the goals, objectives, & milestones (1, 2, & 5 Year)?
- Describe start-Up costs & requirements (Show numbers later)

Marketing Analysis & Competition
- Who is your client/customer base?
- Where are they?
- How do you get them through the door?
- Who is your competition? (Teachers, Studios)
- How do you plan to compete?

The Strategic Plan
- How will the business operate?
- What are your goals and objectives in 1,2 and 5 years?
- What is your competitive edge?
- What is your pricing strategy?
- What is your marketing plan?
- How will you keep growing & innovating the business?

Key Personnel & Background
- Describe key personnel and their background,

Business Risks & Uncertainties
- How stable is pricing in your business?
- How secure is your lease/rent?
- Is your business getting more competitive? Less competitive?
- What happens if you are injured?

Financial Projections & Capital Requirements
- Construct a list of start-up costs
- How will you cover start-up costs?
- Build a financial projections sheet (Income/Expense Yr. 1,2,3)

A Business Plan
For
Ashley Walker – Yoga Instructor

Ashley Walker
1245 Seagull Lane
Bodega Bay, Ca. 94555
Ph. 707-555-5555

Spring 2005

Business Summary

After practicing yoga for seven years, successfully completing two well-regarded teacher-training programs, and filling in as a teacher at my local yoga studio; I am ready to start my own yoga business, "Ashley Walker – Yoga Instructor." Though there are a number of yoga instructors and a yoga studio in my town, no one is teaching the large number of senior citizens that reside here. I plan to build my business by teaching this overlooked group. I have several group contracts as well as private teaching sessions already in place during evenings and the weekends. I plan to build on this base and be teaching yoga as a full time profession within the year. I want to teach yoga and build a reputation as a compassionate, dynamic, and excellent teacher, specializing in the needs of the elderly. My goal is not to open a studio, but to teach small groups and offer private sessions to senior citizens at their homes.

The Company Description & Services

Ashley Walker – Yoga Instructor plans to bring the practice of yoga to a neglected and underserved segment of my community --senior citizens. They will be taught with compassion, attention, and innovation. I will strive to continue my education in yoga, so that I always teach what is most appropriate and safe for my elderly students. I want my teaching reputation to stand for excellence, innovation, and compassion.

Marketing Analysis and Competition

Currently, there is no one teaching yoga to the senior citizens in Bodega Bay, nor am I aware of anyone who is planning to do so. Bodega Yoga (the local studio) has no plans to reach out to the senior groups.

A Business Plan
For
Ashley Walker – Yoga Instructor

The Strategic Plan

My strategic plan is well underway. I have a solid background in my personal yoga practice, teacher-training, and teaching experience. I already have in place, several classes and private sessions during weekdays and weekends at senior facilities. I have plans (as well as student interest) to add additional classes. I have adequate savings. I should be able to be teaching full time in about a year, or whenever I feel financially comfortable in doing so. I will market my services by giving free lectures and demonstrations at lunches and after dinner meetings at various senior residences and community centers.

Key Personnel & Background

I am 31 years old and have been practicing yoga since I was fourteen. I have completed a four-day teaching training at Bodega Yoga, and most recently a three-week teacher training through Forrest Yoga. I have a BA degree from Humboldt State University and am a certified Emergency Medical Technician. I currently work for a private ambulance service.

Business Risks and Uncertainties

From my experience teaching yoga, I feel confident and comfortable that I will love teaching yoga as a career. I can add yoga classes to my work schedule at a rate that is both comfortable and financially sensible. I have savings and a flexible work schedule at my current job. If my yoga business is slower to develop than predicted, I can pick up as much work as I need at the ambulance company.

Financial Projections and Capital Requirements

I am single, with no dependents, and live quite inexpensively. My expenses total about $25,000 a year. I have savings of $50,000, which I am willing to dip into to reach my goal of teaching yoga full time. My work with the ambulance company nets me about $32,000 per year for a 40-hour week. My schedule is flexible, so I can go half-time or quarter-time with the ambulance company if I choose. Starting to teach yoga will increase my expenses as outlined in the income and expense projections below. I can cut back on my ambulance work hours as my teaching schedule increases.

Ashley Walker Yoga Instructor
Financial Projections

	Year 1	Year 2	Year 3
Income			
Classes	2*48*$30= $2,880	4*48*$60=$11,520	6*48*$100=$28,800
Privates	2*48*$60=$5,760	4*48*85=$16,320	6*48*$90=$25,920
Total Income	$8,640	$27,840	$54,720
Expenses			
Auto	$4,000	$5,000	$6,000
Liability Insurance	$200	$200	$200
Health Insurance	$0	$1500	$1500
Phone	$800	$800	$800
Taxes(@ .20 TI)	$1,728	$5,568	$10,944
Clothing	$1,000	$2,000	$2,500
Advertising	$300	$1,000	$1,500
Equipment	$1,000	$1,000	$1,000
Misc.	$200	$1,000	$1,500
Total Expense	$9,228	$17,868	$25,744
Net Pre-Tax Income	$(588)	$9,972	$28,976

** Note that the expenses are for additional yoga teaching expenses, and not personal expenses. Ashley should take those into account, not necessarily here, but in her overall financial picture. On the income lines note that in Year 1 she teaches 2 group classes and 2 private sessions per week. We assume she teaches 48 weeks out of the year and that she receives $30 for each class and $60 for each private sessiond. Notice class numbers and prices go up in years two and three.

GARDEN WAY YOGA

(Business Plan)

The following business plan was provided by Palo Alto Software and is copyrighted by them. I have included it in this book as a sample plan only. There should be no assumption that the advice and information in this plan is reliable, accurate, or suitable for your business.

I gratefully acknowledge and thank Palo Alto Software for granting me permission to use this business plan in this manual and my course. – Art Tiddens, Summer, 2002.

Palo Alto Software has a number of business plans as well as software and assistance for writing business plans. Please check out their site at www.paloalto.com)

Confidentiality Agreement

The undersigned reader acknowledges that the information provided by _____ in this business plan is confidential; therefore, reader agrees not to disclose it without the express written permission of _____.

It is acknowledged by reader that information to be furnished in this business plan is in all respects confidential in nature, other than information which is in the public domain through other means and that any disclosure or use of same by reader, may cause serious harm or damage to _____.

Upon request, this document is to be immediately returned to _____.

_____
Signature

_____
Name (typed or printed)

_____
Date

This is a business plan. It does not imply an offering of securities.

This sample business plan has been made available to users of *Business Plan Pro*™, business planning software published by Palo Alto Software. Names, locations and numbers may have been changed, and substantial portions of text may have been omitted from the original plan to preserve confidentiality and proprietary information.

You are welcome to use this plan as a starting point to create your own, but you do not have permission to reproduce, publish, distribute or even copy this plan as it exists here.

Requests for reprints, academic use, and other dissemination of this sample plan should be emailed to the marketing department of Palo Alto Software at marketing@paloalto.com. For product information visit our Website: www.paloalto.com or call: 1-800-229-7526.

Copyright Palo Alto Software, Inc., 1995-2002

Table of Contents

1. **Executive Summary** 1
    1.1 Objectives 1
    1.2 Mission 2
2. **Company Summary** 2
    2.1 Company Ownership 2
    2.2 Start-up Summary 3
    2.3 Company Locations and Facilities 4
3. **Products and Services** 4
4. **Market Analysis Summary** 5
    4.1 Market Segmentation 5
    4.2 Target Market Segment Strategy 6
    4.3 Service Business Analysis 6
        4.3.1 Competition and Buying Patterns 6
5. **Strategy and Implementation Summary** 7
    5.1 Competitive Edge 7
    5.2 Sales Forecast 7
    5.3 Milestones 8
    5.4 Marketing Strategy 8
6. **Personnel Plan** 8
7. **Financial Plan** 10
    7.1 Break-even Analysis 10
    7.2 Projected Profit and Loss 11
    7.3 Projected Cash Flow 11
    7.4 Projected Balance Sheet 13
    7.5 Business Ratios 13

1.0 Executive Summary

Hatha Yoga is an ancient discipline that explores, develops, and integrates the body, mind, and spirit. Yoga systematically stretches and strengthens muscles throughout the body, increases circulation to internal organs and glands, quiets the nervous system, and improves concentration. This ancient system of self-care brings vitality, health, deep relaxation, and peace of mind.

The style of Hatha Yoga taught is the Anusara method. Anusara Yoga is a new style of yoga that is heart-oriented, spiritually inspiring, yet grounded in a deep knowledge of optimal body alignment in the poses. Instructors encourage students to listen to their body, respect its wisdom, and to progress at their own pace.

Deep relaxation is taught in each class after completion of the postures. The intention of the instructors at Garden Way Yoga Center (GWYC) is to assist students in the development of physical, mental, and spiritual well-being: a truly priceless health advantage.

The Garden Way Yoga Center offers 8 eight-week sessions of classes per year. Courses offered include Anusara-style Hatha Yoga plus workshops in related topics. The Yoga Center features well-trained, professional instructors, progressive teaching methods, a non-competitive and encouraging atmosphere, and a beautiful light-filled facility.

The Garden Way Yoga Center also has a boutique that will sell workshop clothing and yoga training aides.

Jill Gordon, Ph.D., founder of The Garden Way Yoga Center, is one of Anusara Yoga's leading teachers. She conducts workshops and teacher trainings nationally and internationally, and has previously established yoga training centers in Santa Barbara, CA; Denver, CO; and Charlottesville, VA. She co-founded and co-developed the Four Winds Yoga Center in Portland, OR, which offered instruction to nearly 1,000 students per week. She has been a yoga practitioner since 1985 and a meditator since 1989. Jill is a certified Anusara instructor and one of the few Designated Teacher Trainers in the Anusara style of Hatha Yoga. She is registered with the national Yoga Alliance at the highest 500-hour level.

Highlights

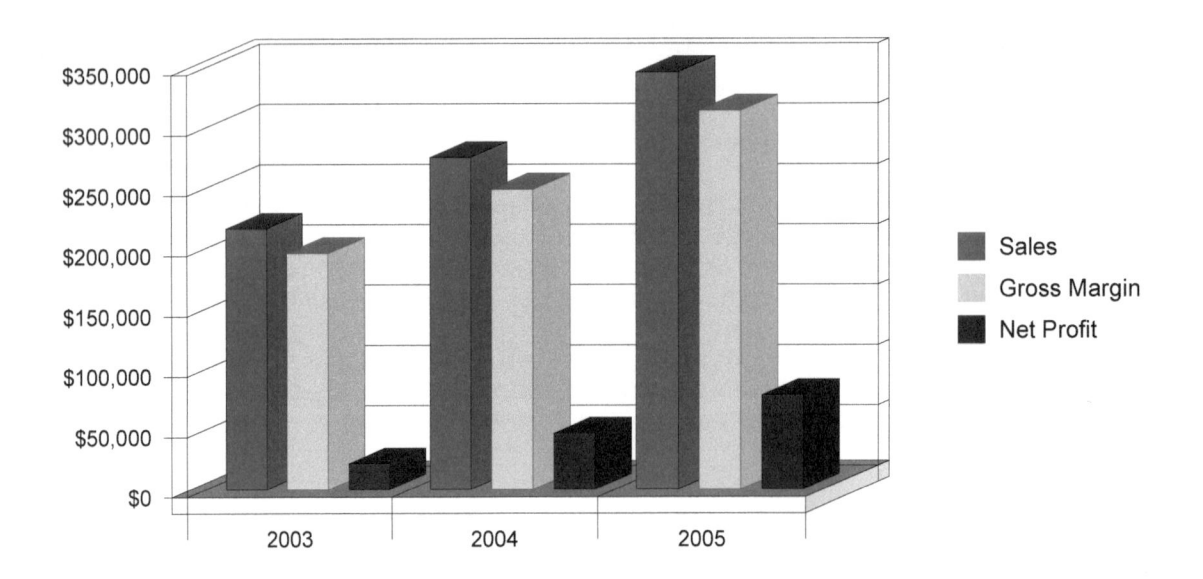

[Bar chart showing Sales, Gross Margin, and Net Profit for 2003, 2004, and 2005. Sales rise from approximately $220,000 in 2003 to $275,000 in 2004 to $350,000 in 2005. Gross Margin rises from approximately $200,000 to $255,000 to $320,000. Net Profit rises from approximately $25,000 to $50,000 to $85,000.]

1.1 Objectives

The objectives of Garden Way Yoga Center are the following:

- Acquire 300 customers by the end of the first year of operation.
- Achieve sales in excess of $60,000 from the boutique.
- Increase customer base by 25% by the end of the second year of operation.
- Increase sales by 15% by the end of the second year of operation.

1.2 Mission

The mission of Garden Way Yoga Center is to give the student, whether a beginner or advanced a place to practice Anusara. It is our intention to keep the teaching of Anusara as close to the way we have been taught as possible. It is incumbent for the teacher to always act responsibly and with the student's interest in mind. No matter what we learn or from whom we learn the real and only teacher is within.

2.0 Company Summary

The Garden Way Yoga Center offers Anusara-style Hatha Yoga plus workshops in related yoga topics. The Yoga Center features well-trained, professional instructors, progressive teaching methods, a non-competitive and encouraging atmosphere, and a beautiful light-filled facility.

GWYC will be located in the commercial downtown section of Monroe, in the renovated Millman Center. GWYC's goal is to build a large base of yoga students from the thousands of office workers that are employed downtown.

Besides the training, the Garden Way Yoga Center also has a boutique that will sell workshop clothing and yoga training aides.

GWYC will operate as a sole proprietorship.

2.1 Company Ownership
The Garden Way Yoga Center is owned by Jill Gordon.

2.2 Start-up Summary

The start-up expenses for the The Garden Way Yoga Center are focused primarily on workshop setup and equipment, and inventory for the boutique and bookstore. Jill will invest $60,000. In addition, GWYC will secure a $80,000 long-term loan.

Table: Start-up

Start-up	
Requirements	
Start-up Expenses	
Legal	$1,000
Stationery etc.	$100
Brochures	$8,000
Insurance	$1,000
Rent	$3,000
Expensed Equipment	$20,000
Total Start-up Expenses	$33,100
Start-up Assets Needed	
Cash Balance on Starting Date	$66,900
Start-up Inventory	$10,000
Other Current Assets	$0
Total Current Assets	$76,900
Long-term Assets	$30,000
Total Assets	$106,900
Total Requirements	$140,000
Funding	
Investment	
Jill Gordon	$60,000
Other	$0
Total Investment	$60,000
Current Liabilities	
Accounts Payable	$0
Current Borrowing	$0
Other Current Liabilities	$0
Current Liabilities	$0
Long-term Liabilities	$80,000
Total Liabilities	$80,000
Loss at Start-up	($33,100)
Total Capital	$26,900
Total Capital and Liabilities	$106,900

Start-up

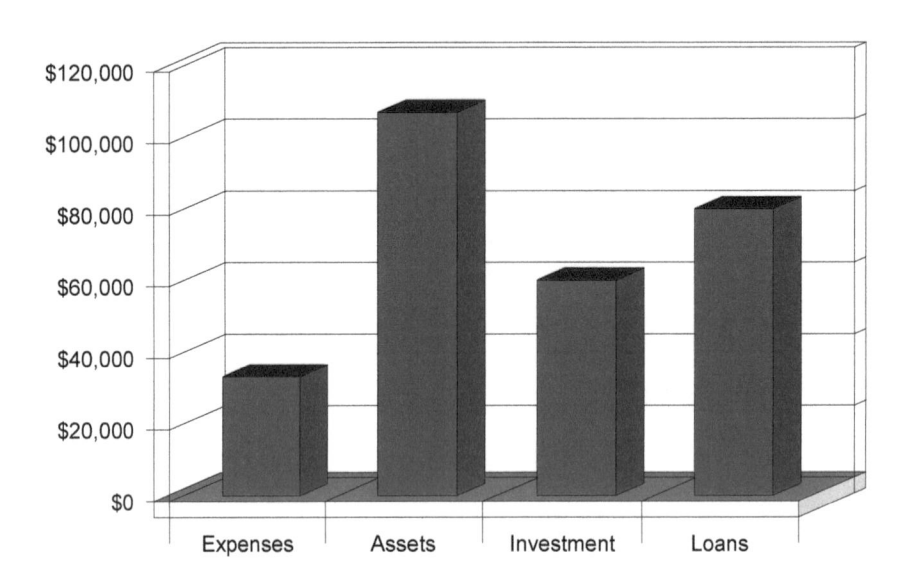

[Bar chart showing: Expenses ~$33,000; Assets ~$108,000; Investment ~$62,000; Loans ~$82,000]

2.3 Company Locations and Facilities

The Garden Way Yoga Center is located in downtown Monroe, in the renovated Millman Center. The facility is quickly accessible to the over 50,000 urban professionals that GWYC considers potential members.

With five large workshop rooms, men and women's dressing rooms, and a boutique, GWYC offers plenty of floor space for multiple classes being conducted simultaneously. In addition, parking is not a problem. GWYC is within easy walking distance from any building in the downtown area. If a customer does decide to drive, the Millman Center has parking space for up to 2,000 vehicles.

3.0 Products and Services

The Garden Way Yoga Center's services and products are as follows:

Services

•**Yoga 1/Beginner** is an introductory class for students who are new to Yoga. This class focuses on poses to stretch and strengthen the legs, back, and shoulders. Emphasis is given to the basic alignment of the standing poses.
•**Fundamentals of Vinyasa Yoga** will prepare students for a vigorous flow style of yoga (Vinyasa) that synchronizes breath with movement. It will offer a balance of strength, flexibility, and endurance to challenge the fitness enthusiast. The course will begin with instruction on the alignment of the poses and move toward linking all the poses together in a continuous flow by the end of the session.
•**Gentle Yoga** is designed for those who prefer a class less vigorous than Yoga 1. It includes gentle stretches and breathing as well as simple movements designed to systematically increase the range of motion of every major joint and increase energy. This class is ideal for students with chronic symptoms such as muscle/joint pain, stiffness, weakness, or fatigue.

- **Yoga 1-2/Continuing Beginner** is a continuation class for Yoga 1. The emphasis of this course is on refining and building endurance in Yoga 1 and Yoga 2 standing poses. It does not include the shoulder stand. The basic Anusara Yoga principles of alignment are presented. This class is suitable for students who have practiced other styles of yoga, but it is not suitable for those who have never studied yoga before.
- **Yoga 2/Intermediate** focuses on refining the standing poses and learning basic sitting postures, simple back bending poses, and the shoulder stand using the Anusara Yoga principles of alignment. It is recommended that students complete both Yoga 1 and Yoga 1-2 before taking Yoga 2.
- **Yoga 3/Advanced** continues with refinements to poses studied in Yoga 2 and introduces full arm balance (handstand), headstand, and forearm balance. Additional back bend poses are also included. Regular yoga practice outside of class is strongly encouraged. Permission of the instructor is required.

Products

- Workshop Clothing: Shirts, shorts, athletic bras and pants.
- Workshop Equipment: Balancing balls, belts, weights, and mats.
- Yoga training aides: Video tapes, instructional manuals, inspirational books.

4.0 Market Analysis Summary

Downtown Monroe has emerged from the recent recession to regain it position as the heart of the city. The growth has been fueled by the increased employment in the city's high tech companies. Currently, 50,000 professional work in downtown Monroe. We believe that a yoga center can be very attractive to our customers if we create a program that fits the time constraints of their jobs. Our location is within easy walking distance from most office buildings downtown. We plan to offer our members a program that will allow them to use their lunch hours to attend workshops.

Jill Gordon will be a positive draw for those who have some experience with yoga instruction. The key to the success of GWYC will be attracting new people to yoga instruction.

4.1 Market Segmentation

The Garden Way Yoga Center will focus on two customer groups:

Middle Income Urban Professionals: This group is the core segment of potential students of GWYC. Their demographic characteristics are the following:

- Ages: 26-40.
- Sex: 30% male, 70% female.
- Family Income: $30,000-$50,000.
- Health/Lifestyle Issues: Active individuals that are focused on healthy food and dieting. Over 70% of this group are members of gyms. Approximately, 40% of potential customers have taken yoga classes before.
- Social Pattern: Will more likely attend as part of group.
- Center's selling point: Close to work. The session lowers stress. Can be attended with workmates as group activity.

Upper Income: The upper income customer is a secondary target group. Their demographic characteristics are the following:

- Ages: 40-60.
- Sex: 30% male, 70% female.
- Family Income: $60,000+.
- Health/Lifestyle Issues: Active individuals that are focused on healthy food and dieting. Over 90% of this group are members of gyms.
- Social Pattern: Will more likely attend alone.
- Center's selling point: Close to work. The session lowers stress.

Table: Market Analysis

Market Analysis Potential Customers	Growth	2002	2003	2004	2005	2006	CAGR
Middle-Income	15%	15,000	17,250	19,838	22,814	26,236	15.00%
High-Income	9%	1,500	1,635	1,782	1,942	2,117	9.00%
Total	14.49%	16,500	18,885	21,620	24,756	28,353	14.49%

Market Analysis (Pie)

4.2 Target Market Segment Strategy

Everything GWYC does must be tailored to work within the time constraints of the target customer. Yoga classes can be no longer than 45 minutes and must be scheduled to fit the break and rolling lunch schedules that exist in the downtown businesses. The focus of the instruction will also have to be tailored to a clientele that will be seeking maximum relief from the pressure of work and then returning to the workplace. If GWYC can create a noticeable difference in the customers' sense of well-being, then the customer will come to depend on instruction as a escape during the day. These kinds of experiences will create a tremendous word of mouth and bring in more first time students.

4.3 Service Business Analysis

Typically, yoga centers are located away from the city's commercial/business center. GWYCs are less focus on serving a large number of beginners and is more focused on obtaining long term students. Students are attracted to a specific type of yoga and the reputation and skills of GWYC's leader.

4.3.1 Competition and Buying Patterns

"Stars do it. Sports do it. Judges in the highest courts do it. Let's do it: that yoga thing. A path to enlightenment that winds back 5,000 years in its native India, yoga has suddenly become so hot, so cool, so very this minute. It's the exercise cum meditation for the new millennium, one that doesn't so much pump you up as bliss you out. Yoga now straddles the continent—from Hollywood, where $20 million-a-picture actors queue for a session with their guru du jour, to Washington, where, in the gym of the Supreme Court, Justice Sandra Day O'Connor and 15 others faithfully take their class each Tuesday morning. "

—***The Power Of Yoga, Time.com*** April 15, 2001

Yoga is a growing trend. It was popular in the seventies and has come back full force into vogue in the 21st century. Movie stars such as Madonna, Meg Ryan, Julia Roberts and Sting are advocates of the discipline.

The key to competition within the yoga business is the quality of the instructor. There are a number of instructors around Monroe who are well respected, and Garden Way Yoga will strive to attract these teachers to its facility. The location, quality and ambiance of the facility is the real competitive advantage for Garden Way. Because it has the best most attractive facility in town teachers will want to teach here and clients will want to "get away" here. Garden Way Yoga Center will focus of presenting GWYC as the perfect place to learn yoga skills that will improve the student physically and reduce the daily stress of the work world.

Other "schools" in the area will be able to match the quality of instruction, but are often held in church halls, community centers, fitness centers, etc. and do not have the relaxing ambiance that is so important to the discipline.

5.0 Strategy and Implementation Summary

The Garden Way Yoga Center will market through the numerous downtown fitness clubs, beauty salons, tanning salons and boutiques. The Garden Way Yoga Center will offer the free open workshop for beginners. In addition, GWYC will initiate a program that will give 25% session discount to members who successfully recruit new members to GWYC.

5.1 Competitive Edge

The competitive advantage of Garden Way Yoga Center is location and the quality and ambiance of the facility. Based in the heart of Monroe, we offer our members excellent instruction that fits into their busy day, providing them a sanctuary from daily pressure. Our facility is a perfect compliment to our brand image.

5.2 Sales Forecast

The sales forecast outlines sales of instruction time as well as sales of products through the boutique located in the facility. Instructions is sold in the following three ways:

1. Private lessons;
2. Eight week courses;
3. Drop-in sessions.

The boutique will sell clothing, books, posters, books, DVDs and videos, mats, and other props for yoga. In addition it will sell healthy prebottled drinks and healthy energy food. In the beginning all food will be pre-packaged, since Jill does not have the facility or expertise to run a cafe facility. If the facility becomes more of a destination, she will research adding a cafe.

The Garden Way Yoga Center anticipates that sales will be slow for the first and second month of operation. After that point, sales will increase as membership grows.

The following is the sales forecast for three years.

Table: Sales Forecast

Sales Forecast			
Sales	2003	2004	2005
Yoga Instruction	$152,000	$190,000	$240,000
Boutique Sales	$64,000	$85,000	$106,000
Other	$0	$0	$0
Total Sales	$216,000	$275,000	$346,000
Direct Cost of Sales	2003	2004	2005
Yoga Instruction	$0	$0	$0
Boutique Sales	$20,150	$26,000	$32,000
Other	$0	$0	$0
Subtotal Direct Cost of Sales	$20,150	$26,000	$32,000

The Business of Yoga

Sales Monthly

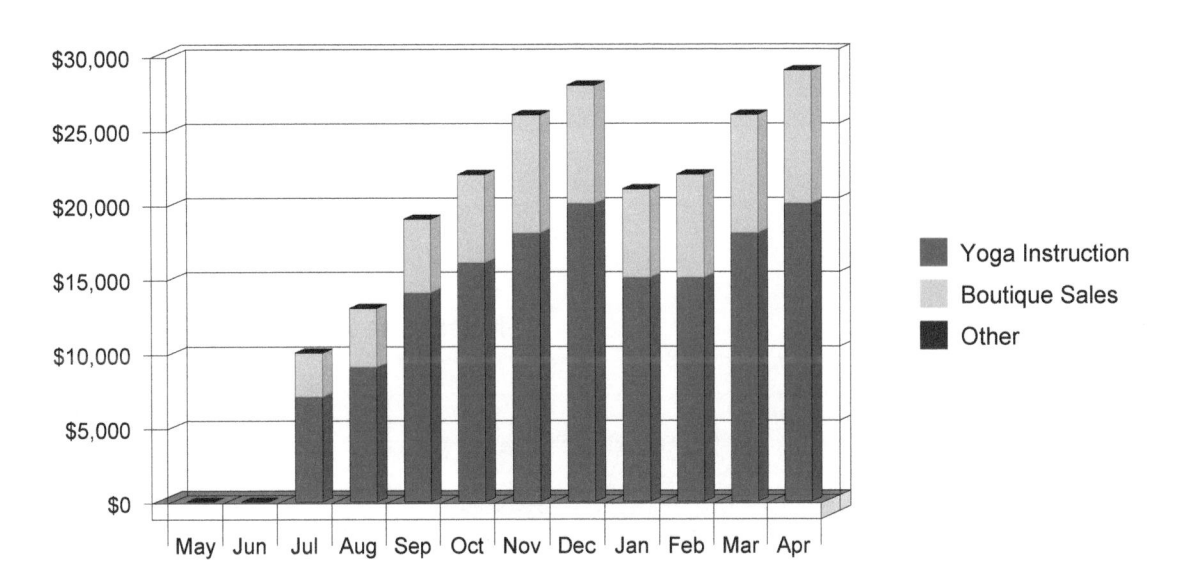

Sales by Year

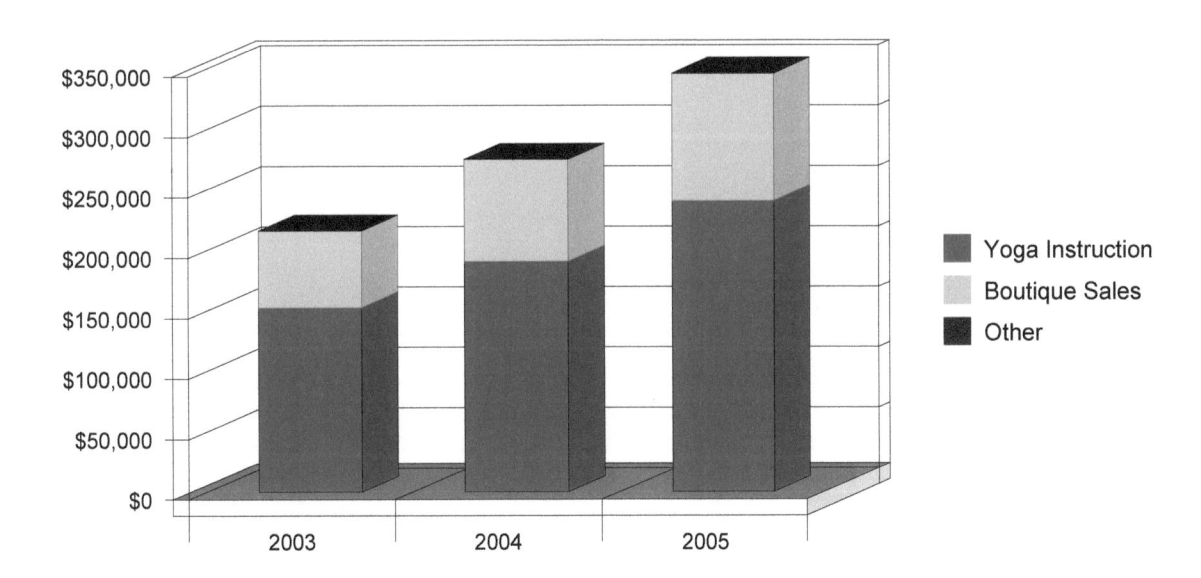

5.3 Milestones

The accompanying table lists important program milestones, with dates and managers in charge, and budgets for each. The milestone schedule indicates our emphasis on planning for implementation.

What the table doesn't show is the commitment behind it. Our business plan includes complete provisions for plan-vs.-actual analysis, and we will be holding follow-up meetings every month to discuss the variance and course corrections.

Table: Milestones

Milestones

Milestone	Start Date	End Date	Budget	Manager	Department
Brochures	3/1/2002	4/23/2002	$8,000	Jill Gordon	
Center Setup	4/16/2002	5/10/2002	$20,000	Jill Gordon	
Marketing Campaign	6/1/2002	7/31/2002	$5,000	Jill Gordon	
Totals			$33,000		

Milestones

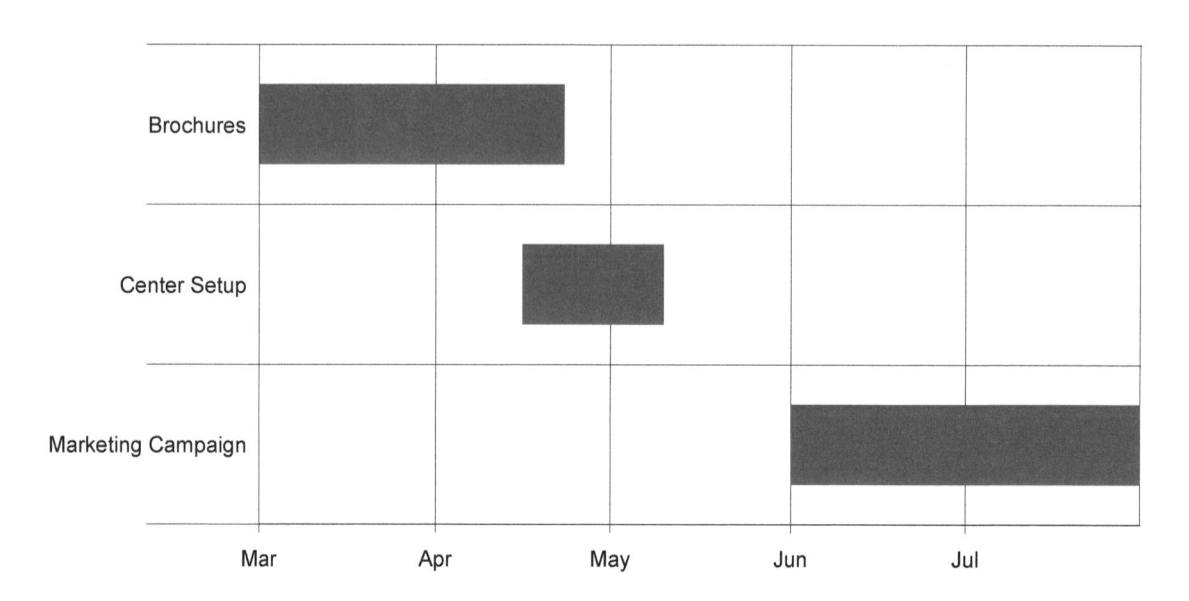

5.4 Marketing Strategy

The key to the marketing strategy is to get the downtown lunch traffic off the streets and into GWYC. GWYC will offer free instruction and will have refreshment available for visitors. The instruction segments will be 45 minutes and focus on exercises that will produce the maximum release of tension.

6.0 Personnel Plan

Jill Gordon, Ph.D., founder of The Garden Way Yoga Center, is one of Anusara Yoga's leading teachers. She conducts workshops and teacher trainings nationally and internationally.

In addition she has excellent business experience having previously established yoga training centers in Santa Barbara, CA; Denver, CO; and Charlottesville, VA. She co-founded and co-developed the Four Winds Yoga Center in Portland, OR, which offers instruction to nearly 1,000 students per week. She has been a yoga practitioner since 1985 and a meditator since 1989.

Jill is a certified Anusara instructor and one of the few Designated Teacher Trainers in the Anusara style of Hatha Yoga. She is registered with the national Yoga Alliance at the highest 500-hour level.

Jill was the business manager Four Winds Yoga Center. GWYC started with four employee and 20 students. Within three years, GWYC had a staff of 25 and over 1,000 students. She was an effective manager of the growth of Four Winds Yoga Center.

The Garden Way Yoga Center's personnel will be the following:

- Jill Gordon, director;
- Teachers (5 half-time);
- Boutique Staff (1).

Table: Personnel

Personnel Plan

	2003	2004	2005
Jill Gordon	$36,000	$36,000	$39,000
Teachers (5)	$54,000	$65,000	$75,000
Boutique Staff	$19,200	$22,000	$25,000
Total People	7	7	7
Total Payroll	$109,200	$123,000	$139,000

7.0 Financial Plan

The following is the financial plan for Garden Way Yoga Center.

7.1 Break-even Analysis

The monthly break-even point is $14,294.

Table: Break-even Analysis

Break-even Analysis:	
Monthly Units Break-even	71
Monthly Revenue Break-even	$14,294
Assumptions:	
Average Per-Unit Revenue	$200.00
Average Per-Unit Variable Cost	$20.00
Estimated Monthly Fixed Cost	$12,865

Break-even Analysis

Monthly break-even point

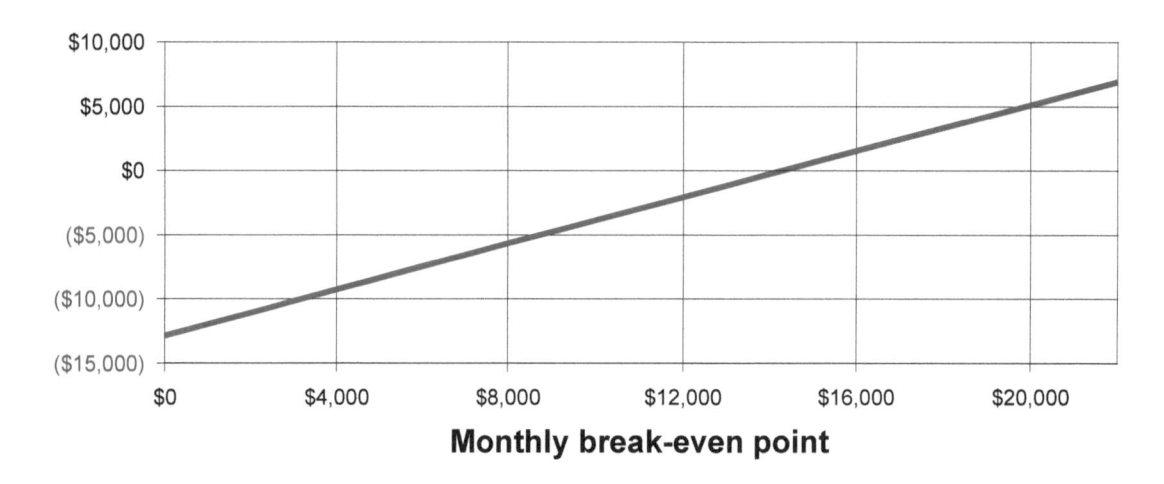

Break-even point = where line intersects with 0

7.2 Projected Profit and Loss

The following table and charts highlight the projected profit and loss for three years.

The Business of Yoga

Table: Profit and Loss

Pro Forma Profit and Loss

	2003	2004	2005
Sales	$216,000	$275,000	$346,000
Direct Costs of Goods	$20,150	$26,000	$32,000
Other Production Expenses	$0	$0	$0
Cost of Goods Sold	$20,150	$26,000	$32,000
Gross Margin	$195,850	$249,000	$314,000
Gross Margin %	90.67%	90.55%	90.75%
Expenses:			
Payroll	$109,200	$123,000	$139,000
Sales and Marketing and Other Expenses	$24,000	$26,000	$28,000
Depreciation	$2,400	$2,400	$2,400
Utilities	$3,300	$3,300	$3,300
Insurance	$2,400	$2,400	$2,400
Payroll Taxes	$16,380	$18,450	$20,850
Other	$0	$0	$0
Total Operating Expenses	$157,680	$175,550	$195,950
Profit Before Interest and Taxes	$38,170	$73,450	$118,050
Interest Expense	$7,721	$7,226	$6,710
Taxes Incurred	$9,135	$19,867	$33,402
Net Profit	$21,315	$46,357	$77,938
Net Profit/Sales	9.87%	16.86%	22.53%
Include Negative Taxes	TRUE	TRUE	TRUE

Profit Monthly

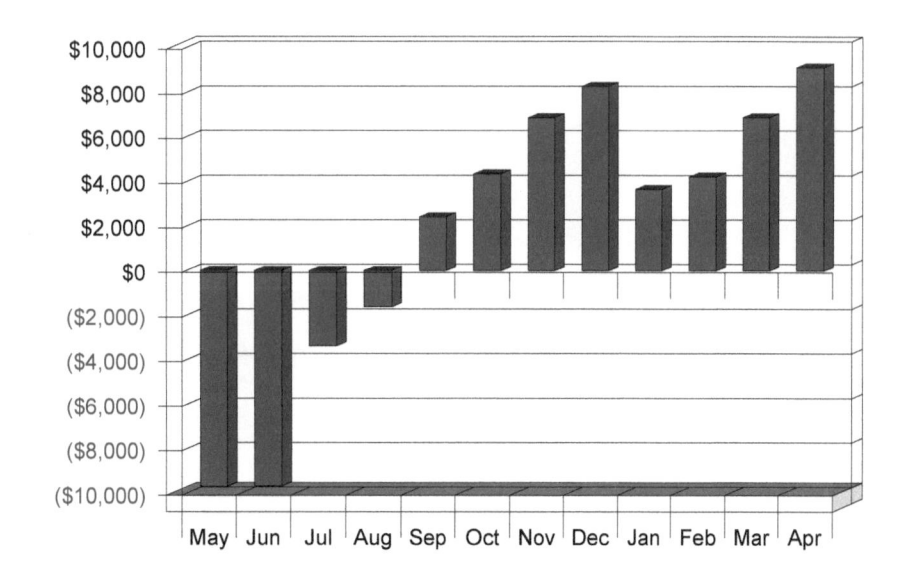

©Astraea Corp. 2005 pg. 55

The Business of Yoga

Profit Yearly

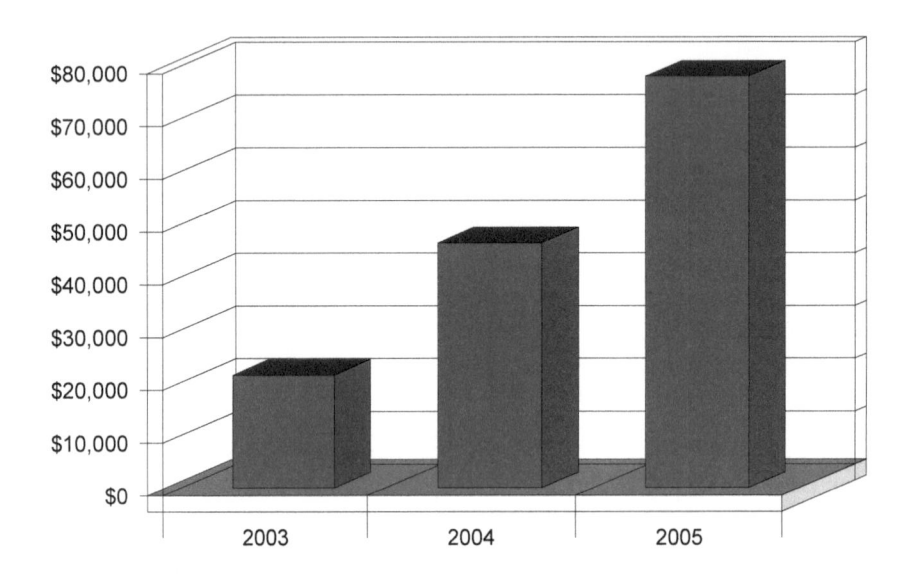

7.3 Projected Cash Flow
The following table and chart highlights the projected cash flow for three years.

Table: Cash Flow

Pro Forma Cash Flow	2003	2004	2005
Cash Received			
Cash from Operations:			
Cash Sales	$216,000	$275,000	$346,000
Cash from Receivables	$0	$0	$0
Subtotal Cash from Operations	$216,000	$275,000	$346,000
Additional Cash Received			
Non Operating (Other) Income	$0	$0	$0
Sales Tax, VAT, HST/GST Received	$0	$0	$0
New Current Borrowing	$0	$0	$0
New Other Liabilities (interest-free)	$0	$0	$0
New Long-term Liabilities	$0	$0	$0
Sales of Other Current Assets	$0	$0	$0
Sales of Long-term Assets	$0	$0	$0
New Investment Received	$0	$0	$0
Subtotal Cash Received	$216,000	$275,000	$346,000
Expenditures	2003	2004	2005
Expenditures from Operations:			
Cash Spending	$5,921	$8,552	$10,656
Payment of Accounts Payable	$169,034	$214,048	$252,257
Subtotal Spent on Operations	$174,954	$222,600	$262,913
Additional Cash Spent			
Non Operating (Other) Expense	$0	$0	$0
Sales Tax, VAT, HST/GST Paid Out	$0	$0	$0
Principal Repayment of Current Borrowing	$0	$0	$0
Other Liabilities Principal Repayment	$0	$0	$0
Long-term Liabilities Principal Repayment	$5,160	$5,160	$5,160
Purchase Other Current Assets	$0	$0	$0
Purchase Long-term Assets	$0	$0	$0
Dividends	$0	$0	$0
Subtotal Cash Spent	$180,114	$227,760	$268,073
Net Cash Flow	$35,886	$47,240	$77,927
Cash Balance	$102,786	$150,026	$227,953

The Business of Yoga

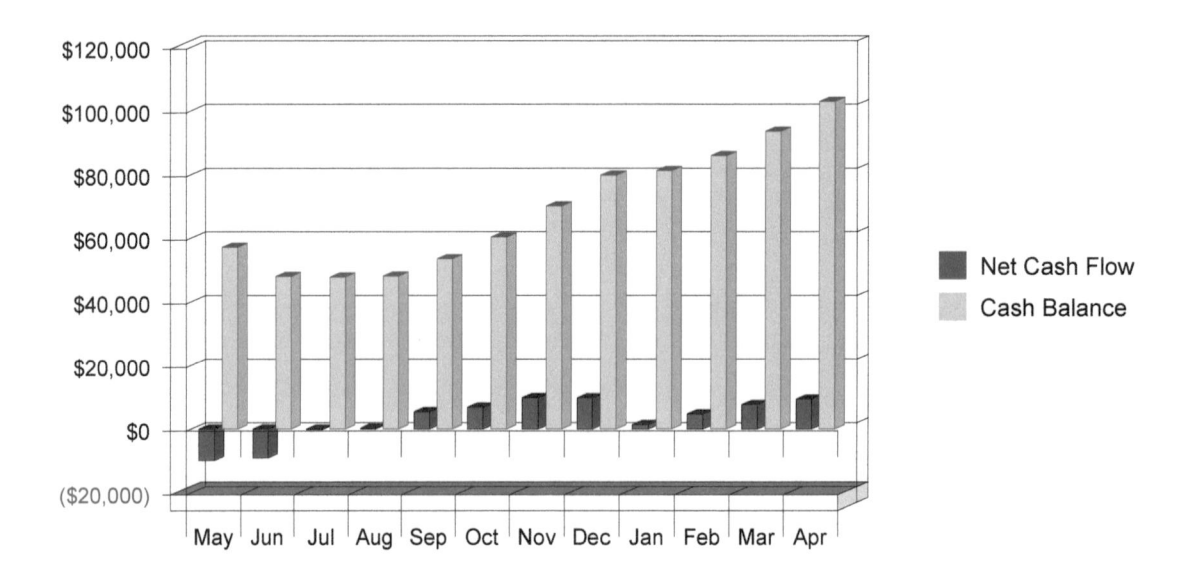

Cash

7.4 Projected Balance Sheet

The following table highlights the projected balance sheet for three years.

Table: Balance Sheet

Pro Forma Balance Sheet

Assets			
Current Assets	2003	2004	2005
Cash	$102,786	$150,026	$227,953
Inventory	$2,500	$3,226	$3,970
Other Current Assets	$0	$0	$0
Total Current Assets	$105,286	$153,252	$231,923
Long-term Assets			
Long-term Assets	$30,000	$30,000	$30,000
Accumulated Depreciation	$2,400	$4,800	$7,200
Total Long-term Assets	$27,600	$25,200	$22,800
Total Assets	$132,886	$178,452	$254,723

Liabilities and Capital			
	2003	2004	2005
Accounts Payable	$9,831	$14,201	$17,694
Current Borrowing	$0	$0	$0
Other Current Liabilities	$0	$0	$0
Subtotal Current Liabilities	$9,831	$14,201	$17,694
Long-term Liabilities	$74,840	$69,680	$64,520
Total Liabilities	$84,671	$83,881	$82,214
Paid-in Capital	$60,000	$60,000	$60,000
Retained Earnings	($33,100)	($11,785)	$34,571
Earnings	$21,315	$46,357	$77,938
Total Capital	$48,215	$94,571	$172,509
Total Liabilities and Capital	$132,886	$178,452	$254,723
Net Worth	$48,215	$94,571	$172,509

7.5 Business Ratios

Business ratios for the years of this plan are shown below. Industry profile ratios based on the Standard Industrial Classification (SIC) code 7997, Membership Sport and Recreation Club, are shown for comparison.

The Business of Yoga

Table: Ratios

Ratio Analysis

	2003	2004	2005	Industry Profile
Sales Growth	0.00%	27.31%	25.82%	15.20%
Percent of Total Assets				
Accounts Receivable	0.00%	0.00%	0.00%	5.10%
Inventory	1.88%	1.81%	1.56%	4.00%
Other Current Assets	0.00%	0.00%	0.00%	31.80%
Total Current Assets	79.23%	85.88%	91.05%	40.90%
Long-term Assets	20.77%	14.12%	8.95%	59.10%
Total Assets	100.00%	100.00%	100.00%	100.00%
Current Liabilities	0.00%	0.00%	0.00%	31.60%
Long-term Liabilities	56.32%	39.05%	25.33%	28.00%
Total Liabilities	56.32%	39.05%	25.33%	59.60%
Net Worth	43.68%	60.95%	74.67%	40.40%
Percent of Sales				
Sales	100.00%	100.00%	100.00%	100.00%
Gross Margin	90.67%	90.55%	90.75%	0.00%
Selling, General & Administrative Expenses	80.80%	73.69%	68.23%	72.30%
Advertising Expenses	2.78%	2.91%	2.89%	2.70%
Profit Before Interest and Taxes	17.67%	26.71%	34.12%	2.60%
Main Ratios				
Current	10.71	10.79	13.11	1.23
Quick	10.46	10.56	12.88	0.83
Total Debt to Total Assets	63.72%	47.00%	32.28%	59.60%
Pre-tax Return on Net Worth	63.15%	70.03%	64.54%	2.80%
Pre-tax Return on Assets	22.91%	37.11%	43.71%	6.90%
Business Vitality Profile	2002	2003	2004	Industry
Sales per Employee	$30,857	$39,286	$49,429	$0
Survival Rate				0.00%
Additional Ratios	2003	2004	2005	
Net Profit Margin	9.87%	16.86%	22.53%	n.a
Return on Equity	44.21%	49.02%	45.18%	n.a
Activity Ratios				
Accounts Receivable Turnover	0.00	0.00	0.00	n.a
Collection Days	0	0	0	n.a
Inventory Turnover	4.04	9.08	8.89	n.a
Accounts Payable Turnover	18.19	15.38	14.45	n.a
Payment Days	11	241	273	
Total Asset Turnover	1.63	1.54	1.36	n.a
Debt Ratios				
Debt to Net Worth	1.76	0.89	0.48	n.a
Current Liab. to Liab.	0.12	0.17	0.22	n.a
Liquidity Ratios				
Net Working Capital	$95,455	$139,051	$214,229	n.a
Interest Coverage	4.94	10.16	17.59	n.a
Additional Ratios				
Assets to Sales	0.62	0.65	0.74	n.a
Current Debt/Total Assets	7%	8%	7%	n.a
Acid Test	10.46	10.56	12.88	n.a
Sales/Net Worth	4.48	2.91	2.01	n.a
Dividend Payout	0.00	0.00	0.00	n.a

PART I WORKSHOP

Here is a chance to work on creating a business plan for opening your own yoga studio or solo teacher business, using your own town, location and special skills or target group. Please try to address all the concerns we have talked about and organize your plan roughly around the structure suggested above. If you can, take a try at some financial projections, going out three years if possible. They can be guesses, and the math doesn't have to be exact. The idea is to get you thinking about <u>all</u> the elements in a business plan. Feel free to refer back to any section that is useful, <u>particularly the business plan checklist on pg. 36.</u>

Part I WORKSHOP (cont.)

Part I WORKSHOP (cont.)

PART II

1.) Getting Going - Where do I go and what do I do when I walk out of Teacher Training?

("Love all, trust a few, do wrong to none." – William Shakespeare, *All's Well That Ends Well*)

Many of you may have this already mapped out, or are going back to existing jobs or businesses. If that's the case please bear with me for a bit. For those of you who want to start teaching — well, this part is specifically for you. I want to walk you through the things you need to think about, and do to start a small business, teaching yoga.

In any case, the idea is to get you going, and most importantly to get you thinking. As with all this material, there are always issues that are particular to your circumstances, items I might not have thought of, and ideas that will come to you as you work through these sections.

As you get your teaching and business going, pay attention to how others do things, but also try to keep an open mind. There are always ways to improve your business, and things to build on from what others have done before you. **Remember, it often takes less time and money to learn from someone else's experiences**.

Once you are back home and settled, I'd let things sit for a bit, resume your normal routine, get back into your personal practice, and think about what you've learned about yourself, your yoga practice, and teaching yoga. Find the time and space within your normal day-to-day routine to think about how and where you might want to teach. Use this manual and the questions, discussions, and steps in it to develop a business plan. **It is essential to develop a long-range plan for your business, but the very first thing is to get out there and teach.**

As we've touched on, there are a number of very good reasons against getting back home, quitting your day job, and going to look for full-time work teaching yoga, or leasing space, or starting your own studio. Presumably, you haven't taught much yoga, if at all, and might not yet have the stamina to teach five classes a day. More than that, you probably won't be able to fill five classes. The odds are that you don't have a reputation as a yoga teacher — yet.

A better approach is to start teaching classes on a part-time basis. Yoga is so popular these days that there are probably more opportunities for teaching in your town then you might be aware of. Besides the studio you practice at, there are probably other studios in town, as well as classes at local health clubs, spas, and hotels. Don't forget the local YMCA. You might also try the local Girls & Boys Clubs, community centers, retirement homes, colleges and universities, and local businesses. Go to as many of these types of classes as you can to see what's out there and how yoga is being taught at the different locations. **This is your market research.** Talk with the instructors, owners, and anyone you can. Those conversations will give you a sense of the yoga business in your community. **Remember to present yourself in the best possible way at each encounter, because in addition to gathering information, you are presenting yourself to your peers and prospective employers, and (indirectly) interviewing for a job**.

(Incidentally, most of these steps apply to any small business. Before you plunge into any business, you may want to work for a competitor or someone in your industry to learn the ropes and see if you like the work. The same is true for getting to know your competition, doing market research, learning about business licenses, appropriate insurance, and the myriad of other details involved in starting a new business. It is easier to learn the ropes by first working for someone else.)

"Being ready" means a lot of things. It does not mean that you'll have your career in yoga all mapped out. It does not mean that you have to take, or will even want, a job if it is offered. ***It does mean* that as you go around, this will be the first time your yoga community will look at you as a prospective teacher.** And the old adage about first impressions holds. What look, impression, and feeling do you want to convey? When trying out different classes, dress appropriately, show up on time or early, and be well scrubbed. Be focused and be professional. If you are certain you want to teach right away---convey that. Be ready if a chance to fill-in or substitute for a teacher comes along. Have business cards and a resume' ready (see below), and know what your schedule is. Remember, this is the time to be as accommodating as possible. If you are not sure about your schedule, be honest. That's acceptable too, as long as you communicate clearly. Don't ever make commitments you cannot keep. <u>**Get professional liability insurance!**</u> (See below)

In my mind, this time is less about finding work, and more about gathering information. Paul Hawken describes information as "nothing more (or less) than how to accomplish something in the best way." That is what you are doing. It is important to get your first teaching job. But filling in at various places around town will give you valuable information about what is being taught, as well as the going rate for your services. You will be learning while you are teaching. Of course, first you have to teach that first class, and you'll need to have business cards and copies of your resume ready to go.

2.) Business Cards & Resume's

(The lucky man is the one who knows how much to leave to chance. -Anonymous)

Trying to change careers and start a new business will put a strain on your personal finances, so being cost-conscious is always a good idea. **Nevertheless, how you present yourself is critical, and passing out business cards and an appropriate resume are key ingredients in creating a favorable first impression.** Remember, they represent you. For both, there are a number of ways to go depending on your budget. There are professionals around that can help you craft cards and resumes, and they are easily found through friends, associates, or a local print shop or stationery store. I'm not sure at this stage the professionals would be necessary. Your local print shop or a *Kinko's* can help you make up inexpensive business cards. There are books and resources (use your local library, if you don't want to buy the books) that can help with writing resumes. The Internet is loaded with self-help sites for both. (I looked on the Internet search engine *Google* and found dozens of resume writing sites (many of them free), and a search at *Amazon.com* turned up 280 books on writing resumes. It's a cottage industry.)

Business cards should look clean (not too busy), and contain <u>essential</u> and <u>reliable</u> contact information. They can and should be creative, *but must be easy to read. Especially if your prospective clients are older.* (I have a card from a graphic artist that you have to hold in front of a light to read. The effect is dramatic, but it's hard to see the phone number in low light and that can be annoying.

Don't put down any information on your business card that is not reliable. For example, don't print your friend's address on the card if you are only staying there a month. In fact, if you move around a lot get a Post Office box or mailbox at Mailboxes etc or an equivalent. But don't go to the trouble of renting one unless you are going to check it on a regular basis. These days many people have cell phones and e-mail. It is acceptable to put these on your business cards. In fact, they are much better choices than an answering machine shared by three people, or an address that may not remain current. As a teacher, you may not want your home address on your business card.

Ashley's card might read: Ashley Walker   Certified Yoga Instructor, followed by her address and phone number. A word about your teaching style or method is appropriate too. Ashley's might say, "Special Practice for Senior Citizens." Always make sure that the phone number you give out is working and has voice mail with a clear, short message. **Make sure you return messages within 24 hours or sooner.** Don't put down multiple phone numbers, if you are not willing to retrieve messages from all of them regularly. One contact number is also less confusing. Don't put down an e-mail address if you change them frequently, or if you don't check and reply to e-mails at least once a day.

Before you make up your business card, collect business cards from all sorts of professionals and businesses. Study them and think about what strikes you immediately; notice what you like and dislike.

Resume's should be along the same lines. They need to convey the necessary information in a clear and concise fashion. They must be easy to read. Fancy or stylized fonts defeat themselves if they are not easy on the eye. The point of a resume' is to introduce yourself on paper. It should explain who you are, what you're looking for, and outline your qualifications and experience for the job. Two sample resumes' follow. Note the essential items they share. While resume' writing is almost an industry in itself, I don't think one way is necessarily better than another. One page is great, if you can accomplish what you need; use two pages if you must. Don't write a book-- it won't be read. You should be ready with additional information in an organized format if someone asks for the "long version" of your resume'. You want your resume' to be eye-catching, informative, clean, and concise.   You want it to get you the job.

Use a good quality paper on both cards and resume's.

Two books that may be of some help are: *The Resume' Handbook: How to Write Oustanding Resumes and Cover Letters for Every Situation,* Arthur D. Rosenberg and David V. Hizer. *Resume Writing: A Comprehensive how-to-do-it Guide*, Burdette E. Bostwick. And don't forget to look on the Internet.

Look over the resume' that follows and see if it accomplishes what we have talked about. What stands out? What don't you like?

Add to your planning checklist:

Do I have business cards and an appropriate resume ready to go?

The Business of Yoga

(NAME GOES HERE)

327 Conejo Road ■ Santa Barbara, CA 93103 : (PHONE & E MAIL GO HERE)

PROFILE

Dynamic and joyful yoga teacher with 14 years of yoga experience. Knowledgeable in Hatha, Iyengar, Vinyasa, Power, Bikram and Kripalu. Additionally, 12 years of vipassana meditation experience. Prefer to work with beginner and intermediate students focusing on breathing exercises and asanas to energize the body, relax the mind, and free the spirit.

YOGA TEACHER TRAINING AND EXPERIENCE

- **Forrest Yoga Teacher Training** with yoga master, **Ana Forrest**, Seattle, WA — 2001
- **Yoga Anatomy and Physiology Workshop** with Chiara Guerrieri, LMP, Seattle, WA — 2001
- Taught **Beginner's Workshop** collaboratively with Ana Forrest, Seattle, WA — 2001
- Studied under the guidance of nationally and internationally recognized teachers including:
    - **Cindy Lee** and Dana Strong of **OM Yoga** in New York, NY
    - **Baron Baptiste** of **Baptiste Power Yoga** in Cambridge, MA
    - **Beverley Murphy** and Rachel Zinnman of **Yoga Zone** in New York, NY
    - Melina Meza of **8 Limbs Yoga** in Seattle, WA

EDUCATION

B.A., Anthropology and Pre-Medicine, **cum laude**
Minor in Culture, Health and Science
Mount Holyoke College, South Hadley, MA — 1999

PROFESSIONAL EXPERIENCE

Columbia Presbyterian Hospital, Office of Complementary Medicine, New York, NY — 1998
A recognized worldwide leader in academic medicine and the provision of excellent, innovative medical care.

Research Assistant Summer Intern

Collaborated in a research project that focused on finding herbal remedies for menopausal women
- Utilized Internet search engines, such as Medline, to perform medical research
- Prepared summaries of submitted medical papers and assisted in organizing medical research

Service Net, Inc., Northampton, MA — 1995–1997
A non-profit outpatient mental health organization providing a full continuum of behavioral health and social services.

Office Manager/Intake Coordinator, Adult Outpatient Clinic (1996-1997)

Managed and supervised the operations of a busy outpatient psychiatric clinic, including acting as a liaison between management, billing department, clinical staff, and psychiatric staff
- Contributed to the development of new strategies for decreasing operating expenses, and corporate financial deficit

Receptionist, Adult Outpatient Clinic (1995-1996)

Promoted from Receptionist to Office Manager/Intake Coordinator within first 6 months

ADDITIONAL PROFESSIONAL EXPERIENCE

Ray & Berndtson, Inc., New York, NY — 2000-2001
Knowledge Specialist, Financial Services

Heidrick & Struggles, New York, NY — 2000
Executive Assistant, Financial Services

3.) Approaching Businesses (The Interview)

("Fortune favors the brave – Virgil)

An interview can be nerve-racking, if you haven't interviewed for a while, but it should not be. Yoga is extremely popular these days, and clubs, studios, and other places that offer yoga are always on the lookout for new teachers, especially well-qualified ones. Once you have taken several classes at a location where you would like to teach, introduce yourself to the manager or owner (find out who hires the yoga teachers), and ask: "may I have fifteen minutes of your time — *at your convenience?*"

In your one-on-one meeting you might present yourself this way: *"I have just finished teacher training and am looking at all the yoga studios, clubs and other places in town where I might like to teach. I would very much like to teach at this center, and would like to talk with you about that. I am available at these times and I would like to leave my resume' and business card with you."*

You might emphasize that you are willing to fill in for teachers on short notice, and would be happy to audition if that is appropriate. If the person does not know about your particular teacher training program, take some time to talk a bit about that. Before you contact and meet with these people, ask yourself, "If I were they, what would I like to see from a prospective teacher/employee?" Ask other students and teachers about their interviewing experience (on either side of the table).

Once you start getting recognized as a yoga teacher in your community, opportunities will come your way, especially if you are committed to working, whenever work is offered. **This is the time to build those first impressions into a reputation as a yoga instructor who is willing to work, and is a professional in all respects.** Be recognized as the new teacher who is willing to substitute on short notice, or acknowledged as the new teacher with boundless energy and lots of new ideas. Or perhaps as the new teacher who has awakened the sleepy yoga class at the YMCA, and turned it into the most popular event at the center. These first few months will have a lot to do with your reputation as a yoga teacher in your community. **Be mindful of your presentation, your work, your attitude, and your focus**.

Most studios hire teachers on an "independent contractor" basis. This is normal and helps them avoid all the paperwork and hassle of taking on full-time employees. I've included a sample independent contractor agreement following page 70.

Also, learn as much as you can. Spend extra time learning how things work around the studio. What you learn will be invaluable later on if you open your own business.

One routine to be very aware of is taking care of classroom paperwork (the intake forms, class registration, release forms, pre-existing health conditions, etc.) correctly. **If you feel there are omissions, or you are unclear on any issues---ask, especially on any insurance matters, or issues concerning the safety or health of your students**. For example, it may not occur to the community center that wants you to start a yoga class that release forms are necessary or that their insurance might not cover yoga classes. It is always better to ask and be certain.

For any class that you teach, in any location, whether you volunteer or do it for pay, whether it is 30 students or a single private student, your students need to sign an Agreement of Release & Waiver of Liability.

As you know, you need to be aware of each student's medical history and previous injuries. Always remember that you are a yoga instructor, not a therapist, not a doctor. Particularly with private sessions, don't offer any advice outside of your professional training.

Take a look at the following sign-in and release forms. (Also included is a policy and guideline form. You might want to develop one of your own.) In each case, there is a place for the student to sign acknowledging the risks inherent in yoga, and that he or she assumes those risks. I suspect ten different lawyers would come up with ten different forms (anybody can sue over anything, regardless, it seems, of what they sign) but it is important to have some kind of signed acknowledgment, in any case.

In your business planning checklist ask yourself:

How do I want to present myself to the yoga community and at job interviews?

Does my studio (or do I) have an appropriate sign-in and release sheet?

Independent Contractor Agreement

This agreement is made between **XYZ Yoga Center** hereafter referred to as the "Client" and **Ashley Walker**, herein referred to as the "Contractor." This agreement is entered into in Bodega Bay, California, and shall be performed in Bodega Bay, among other places.

Terms of the Contract

This agreement will begin on _____, and will continue until cancelled by either party or until _____. Either party can cancel this contract with 90 days written notice. The Contractor shall choose his schedule at the Client's center, and the Client shall make a general schedule containing all of the Contractors' classes available to the public. Once on the schedule, the Contractor is obligated to teach his scheduled classes or provide a suitable and qualified substitute. In the event these obligations are not met, the Client is entitled to compensation for up to one month's lost revenue of the average monthly income for the Contractor's relevant class or classes,

Contractor Services

The Client operates a yoga studio and is hiring the Contractor to teach yoga classes. In doing so, the Contractor is responsible for teaching yoga classes and providing qualified substitute teachers and assistants as needed at the Contractor's expense.

Further, the Contractor warrants that he posses the knowledge and training requisite to his job. The Contractor will have sole discretion in determining the methods and details in teaching his class. The Contractor will comply with all local, state, and federal laws. The Contractor is responsible for the marketing and advertising of his classes. The Contractor will supply all necessary equipment for his classes. The Contractor shall have liability insurance that is current and in force.

Client Services

The Client shall comply with all local, state, and Federal laws. The Client shall provide a safe, dry, and appropriately heated studio in which the Contractor teaches his classes. The Client shall provide changing areas, waiting areas, and restrooms for students that use the facility. The Client's studio shall be in compliance with all building and zoning codes. The Client shall have adequate liability insurance that is current and in force.

Independent Status of Contractor

The Contractor is an independent contractor and is not an employee, nor has any business relationship with the Client, other than stated in this contract. The Client shall have no obligation to pay any employment taxes, or any other job related fees, taxes, or benefits on behalf of the Contractor.

The Contractor is free to pursue work in the yoga field independent of the Client's studio, and the Client shall have no control, nor any financial interest in these pursuits.

The Contractor warrants that he has and will keep current and in force his own liability insurance while working for the Client.

The Contractor agrees to maintain Worker's Compensation Insurance, while working for the Client, if required by law.

The Contractor agrees to have all required business licenses, fictitious business statements, and other forms that may be required, while working for the Client.

The Client withholds no taxes on behalf of its Contractors. The Contractor is responsible and liable for all taxes due as a result of the Contractor's compensation.

Compensation

The Contractor will be paid on a monthly basis for his services, at the rate of _____ per _____ (ex. Student/class). The Contractor will not be paid for guests of the Contractor or employees of the Client, as long as the Guests and employees of the Client participate in the Contractor's classes on a space available basis.

The Business of Yoga

dogtree yoga

Suite #250
967 E. Parkcenter Blvd.
Boise, Idaho 83706
www.dogtreeyoga.com
208/890.4361

Sign in Sheet for Class

Class Date: _____   Class Time: _____

Yoga Instructor's Name: _____

Please Print Clearly

Participants Names:

1. _____   16. _____
2. _____   17. _____
3. _____   18. _____
4. _____   19. _____
5. _____   20. _____
6. _____   21. _____
7. _____   22. _____
8. _____   23. _____
9. _____   24. _____
10. _____   25. _____
11. _____   26. _____
12. _____   27. _____
13. _____   28. _____
14. _____   29. _____
15. _____   30. _____

peace, love, and tranquility   gratitude, loving kindness, and compassion

The Business of Yoga

Agreement of Release and Waiver of Liability

dogtree yoga

Suite #250
967 E. Parkcenter Blvd.
Boise, Idaho 83706
www.dogtreeyoga.com
208/890.4361

I, _____, hereby agree to the following:

1. I am participating in the Yoga Classes, Health Programs or Workshops offered by DogTree Yoga and/or heather Van Houten during which I will receive information and instruction about yoga and health. I recognize that yoga requires physical exertion which may be strenuous and may cause physical injury, and I am fully aware of the risks and hazards involved.
2. I understand it is my responsibility to consult with a physician prior to and regarding my participation in the Yoga Classes, Health Programs or Workshops. I represent and warrant that I am physically fit and I have no medical condition which would prevent my full participation in the Yoga Classes, Health Programs or Workshops.
3. In consideration of being permitted to participate in the Yoga Classes, Health Programs or Workshops, I agree to assume full responsibility for any risks, injuries or damages, known or unknown, which I might incur as a result of participating in the program.
4. In further consideration of being permitted to participate in the Yoga Classes, Health Programs or Workshops, I knowingly, voluntarily and expressly waive any claim I may have against DogTree Yoga and/or heather Van Houten for injury or damages that I may sustain as a result of participating in the program.
5. I, my heirs or legal representatives forever release, waive, discharge and covenant not to sue DogTree Yoga and/or heather Van Houten for any injury or death caused by their negligence or other acts.

I have read the above release and waiver of liability and fully understand its contents. I voluntarily agree to the terms and conditions stated above.

Date _____ Signature of Participant _____

If participant is under 18:

As legal guardian of _____, I consent to the above terms and conditions.

Date _____ Signature of Guardian _____

Witnessed by: _____

peace, love, and tranquility   gratitude, loving kindness, and compassion

©Astraea Corp. 2005 pg. 74

The Business of Yoga

Yoga with heather Van Houten Registration and Attendance Record

Please Print Clearly

Name: _____
Home phone: _____
Work phone: _____
email: _____
Address: _____
City: _____ State: _____ Zip code: _____
Occupation: _____
How did you hear of these yoga classes? _____
Yoga Background: _____
Emergency Contact: _____ Phone: _____
Injuries/Medical History: _____
_____
_____
_____
_____
_____
_____

If more space is needed use the back of this document.

Please Read Carefully:
I am aware that heather Van Houten is here to serve me by sharing knowledge of Hatha Yoga and health. By my participation in classes or activities by heather Van Houten, I agree to take full responsibility for not exceeding my limits in the practice of yoga and for any injury I might suffer in the practice of yoga. It is my responsibility to ascertain that there is no medical reason to prevent my participation. In consideration for heather Van Houten's yoga operations, I waive any claim that I might have at any time for injury of any sort against heather Van Houten or any person or entity in any way involved therewith. This release waives the provisions set out in Idaho Civil Code, which provides a general release does not extend to claims which the creditor does not know to exist in his favor at the time of executing the release, which if known to him must have materially affected his settlement with the debtor. I do hereby waive and relinquish all rights and benefits I have or may have under this Civil Code of the State of Idaho to the full extent that that I may lawfully waive all rights and benefits pertaining to the subject matter of this Agreement for which a release has been given. I have carefully read the release, fully understand and agree to the above.

Date _____

Signature of Participant _____

967 E. Parkcenter Blvd. No. 250
Boise, Idaho 83706
hvh_3bdog@yahoo.com
208) 890-4361

©Astraea Corp. 2005 pg. 75

heather Van Houten

Policies and Guidelines

Hygiene
- Come to class clean, keep your feet clean
- Do not wear perfume/cologne
- Wear clean clothes, dress comfortably - avoid zippers and loose short shorts - were cloths that are comfortable and allow you to move and twist - do not were cloths that you are falling out or hanging out - if in doubt, don't wear it!
- Leave jewelry off

Time
- Arrive early in order to have time to prepare your space and discuss any injuries you may have with instructor
- Available time after class to ask questions pertaining to the class work or yoga

Communication
- Please do not hold conversations with your neighbor(s) during class, excessive talk disrupts the flow of the class and makes it hard to hear instruction

Boundaries
- Respect each other's space in the class
- Honor yourself when participating in yoga
- Do not harm yourself or others during your time at the Broadway Dance Center

Policies
- Be on time to class, we start on time
- Sessions must be paid for in advance, for questions call heather
- No refunds for classes or sessions not attended, no exceptions made

967 E. Parkcenter Blvd. No. 250
Boise, Idaho 83706
hvh_3bdog@yahoo.com
208) 890-4361

4.) Insurance

("Better safe than sorry" – often said, but sadly true, at least regarding insurance)

This is one area, no matter what your budget, where you need to spend money, and immediately. **Get good liability insurance for teaching yoga from a reliable company**. I would highly recommend getting it before you start teaching-- even if you are teaching part time. While some studios will provide insurance for you when you teach classes, it is still a good idea to have your own in place. That way, if a policy at a small center you teach at doesn't cover you, or it lapses because they forget to pay it, or you're invited to teach a private lesson on short notice---you are covered.

I recently talked with a friend who is teaching yoga in Santa Barbara. She took her teacher training three years ago, knows all about her insurance options, and has yet to purchase a policy. I think it's a big mistake. It only takes one incident-- one accident—to ruin you financially. And as you will see below, good coverage costs only about $200 per year.

Another friend is an acupuncturist. About a month after graduating, she was working part-time at a clinic, helping out. It would seem that there is little you could do with a small acupuncture needle, but she somehow managed to puncture a lung, and deflate it. While not life threatening, the incident was scary, incredibly painful for the patient, and resulted in a 911 call and an emergency room procedure. My friend wasn't sued (fortunately), but the medical bills were about $2,000. **Even if you have no assets, you still have future earnings that could be attached. Get insurance!**

IMA (International Massage Association) offers insurance to yoga instructors through their Yoga Division. Their phone number is 540-351-0800, and they are on the web at www.IMAGroup.com. IMA offers good coverage (for up to 99 students per class), for professional, general, and personal injury liability insurance at around $200 per year. California Yoga Teachers Association offers similar coverage. Their number is 800-395-8075. (Additional information follows.) Check the Yoga Journal or similar publications for other companies that offered insurance.

Insurance is the very first thing your new business should spend money on. Get it early and you will be ready for any opportunities that come along.

Your checklist question:

Do I have adequate yoga liability insurance from a reliable company?

IMA Group

The Information Brochure For

Yoga™

IMA Group
Yoga Division

25 South Fourth Street
PO Drawer 421
Warrenton, VA 20188
(540) 351-0800

What is the IMA Group?

We are a group of trade associations which currently include eleven divisions in the natural health field. The IMA Group was formed April 1, 1994. To date, over 39,000 people have joined. The president of the group, Will Green, has more than 20 years of experience in the massage and fitness industry.

Mission Statement

The IMA Group is committed to developing a group of affiliated trade associations that become a positive force in their fields; gaining success, acceptance and respect for the professions and the individual practitioners. We intend to accomplish these goals by providing our members with liability insurance, access to information, networking opportunities and requiring high business standards as defined in our Code of Ethics.

Frequently Asked Questions

What does the IMA insurance cover? The IMA Group policy is liability insurance. It covers damage done to other people and other people's property, not our member's property. It covers malpractice, which includes professional and general liability, and it covers the oils you put on clients as well as fire damage to the building you are working in.

What are the limits of my coverage? Professional liability limits alone are $2,000,000 per occurrence and $2,000,000 aggregate (total per year). Your total coverage is $5,000,000 aggregate. This information is detailed on the back of the application.

How do I know that the insurance company is good? The IMA Group buys your insurance from a domestic company which is listed in the A.M. Best book rating insurance companies. This company has the highest possible rating, A++ Superior.

What do I do if I have a claim? Call the IMA Group immediately and we will send you a claim form. The sooner we know about a situation, the better.

If I travel to other states am I covered? You are covered in all 50 states as well as all US Territories as long as you obey the local laws. Be sure you have the required license for the area you are working in.

Can I join or renew my membership over the phone? No. We must have in writing authorization to join or to renew membership for our files.

What do I get with my membership? You will receive a Certificate of Insurance (Practicing members only), Wall Certificate, Wallet Card and an IMA Group information packet fully explaining your benefits.

The Business of Yoga

The IMA Group

(540) 351-0800 phone (540) 351-0816 fax
Office Hours: 9:00-5:00 Eastern Time M-F

The Eleven Associations of the IMA Group

Yoga, Aromatherapy, Movement, Reflexology, Massage, Massage & Movement Schools, Colonic Educators, Kinesiology, Feng Shui, Dance Teachers & Estheticians

Qualifications for Membership

30 hours minimum training by either an approved apprenticeship or school are required. You must also obey the local laws where you are practicing.

Modalities

Hatha
Iyengar
Jivamukti
Kripalu
Power Yoga
Raja
Tai Chi

Ashtanga
Tantra
Sivananda
Jois
Kundalini
Chi Kung
etc...

About the Application

The application is a legal document that the IMA Group needs on file. It is important that all information is accurate, complete and legible. Please list your legal name and the address you wish your packet to be delivered. Telephone numbers are important in case we need to contact you—please include both home and business numbers. Your Social Security number is important for insurance purposes. If you were referred by someone please include their name on the referral line. The yearly rate for Associate Membership (without insurance) is $79. This membership includes all benefits listed except insurance. For Practicing Membership (with insurance) the yearly rate is $129. This also provides coverage to teach 1-9 students. To be covered to teach 10-99 students, membership with insurance is $229.

Copy of Policy:
This is a 40 page master policy and is an extra $10 charge if ordered. You may review the policy before joining for the same $10 fee (to cover printing and postage). Sorry—no exceptions

Fax Service:
A Certificate of Insurance is included in your membership packet, however, if there is a rush we can fax this to you for an additional charge of $10.

Next Day Air:
If you are in a rush to receive your entire membership packet we can send your materials next-day-air by UPS for an additional $30 charge.

Post Company Name on Internet:
If you have your own company and wish to list your company name on the internet, check the appropriate box and enclose an additional $10 fee.

Post Techniques on the Internet:
You may list up to 3 techniques on the internet for a $10 charge or 4 to 7 techniques for $20.

Certificate Holder/Additional Insured:
If you need to add an Additional Insured (i.e., landlord, employer) list the name and complete street address on the back of the application (P.O. Boxes are not acceptable). There is an extra $10 charge per Additional Insured or Certificate Holder.

Benefits

• **Coverage Includes All Divisions Except Estheticians**
Membership in the Yoga division of the IMA Group provides liability coverage to practice other modalities including Movement, Massage, Aromatherapy, Reflexology, Feng Shui, Colonic Educators, Kinesiology and Dance. You are covered to teach up to 9 students in any of these modalities. To be covered to teach 10-99 students, membership with insurance is $229. If you are also a Licensed Esthetician, and wish to have coverage as an Esthetician in addition to Yoga, you may upgrade your policy by submitting an additional fee. Please contact an IMA Group representative for further details.

• **Free Internet Referral Service**
Your name and business number will be listed on our website free of charge. Our web address is *www.imagroup.com*.

• **Optional Health Coverage**
Take advantage of this comprehensive and affordable health care program that is available to all IMA Group members.

• **Optional Business Property Coverage**
Cover your business equipment through the same company that provides your liability coverage. Rates vary with amount of coverage.

• **IMA Success Newsletter**
You will receive periodic issues of *IMA Success*.

• **Credit Card Merchant Account**
Accept major credit cards and your business will blossom. Clients appreciate the convenience of paying by credit card. Special member rates are available.

• **Job Placement Service**
Looking for a job? Check out our members-only Job Placement Service on the IMA Group website.

• **Discount Long Distance Service**
Decrease your monthly bills with this discount phone service available to IMA Group members.

• **Customer Service**
The IMA Group staff is in the office from 9-5 Eastern Time Monday-Friday. We are happy to answer your questions or provide assistance at any time during these hours.

©Astraea Corp. 2005 pg. 79

The Business of Yoga

★★ JOIN ★★ JOIN ★★ JOIN ★★ JOIN ★★ JOIN ★★ JOIN ★★ JOIN ★★ JOIN ★★

INTERNATIONAL YOGA ASSOCIATION

MEMBERSHIP APPLICATION

International Yoga Association
25 South Fourth Street • P.O. Drawer 421
Warrenton, VA 20188-0421
(540) 351-0800
(540) 351-0816 fax (available 24hrs.)
www.imagroup.com

Please print or type all information • Incomplete applications will not be processed • Please allow one week for processing

Mr. ☐ Ms. ☐ _____ First _____ Last _____ Social Security #: _____
Mailing Address: _____
City _____ State/Province _____ Zip _____ Country: _____
Home phone #: (___) _____ Phone # For Free Web Listing: (___) _____
Date of Birth: ___/___/___ Referred by: _____ Name _____ Membership Number
Years in Practice: _____ E-Mail: _____
Training: ☐ School: _____ (For those who attended a formal school) ☐ Apprenticeship: _____ (The person you learned from, if not a formal school)

By my signature below I understand that upon acceptance as an IMA member, all fees paid by me to the IMA are non-refundable. I hereby state that I have no knowledge of any incident, pending claims, suits, or ethics violations nor have any been filed against me in the past pertaining to my practice as a massage/movement practitioner, that no massage/movement license, registration or certification has been revoked, that no disciplinary action has been or is pending against me, and that I have never been arrested for or been charged with any sexual violations. I understand that there is no insurance coverage provided for psychological and related therapies, or any massage/movement using implements other than the body. Manipulations or adjustments of the human skeletal structure, diagnosis, prescriptions, or any other service, procedure or therapy that requires a license to practice chiropractic, osteopathy, physical therapy, podiatry, orthopedics, or any other profession or branch of medicine is excluded. I understand that insurance is issued upon underwriter's approval, and that my signature shall verify that I have completed the IMA membership application accurately and honestly. I understand that any false statement made on this application or subsequent renewals shall void this application, terminate my membership, render my insurance coverage null and void (if applicable), and I may be subject to further legal action. Returned checks will be charged a $25.00 administrative fee.

Signature **(REQUIRED)** _____ Date _____

Because a signature is required, no application can be accepted over the phone.
• Apply by FAX with a credit card or by MAIL with check, money order or credit card •

☐ $79 for a 1 year Associate Membership WITHOUT INSURANCE .... $ _____
☐ $129 for a 1 year Practicing Membership WITH INSURANCE (Includes coverage to teach 1-9 students) ... $ _____
  ☐ *Large Class Option:* Add $100 to include coverage to teach classes of 10-99 students ... $ _____
  ☐ *Additional Coverage Option:* Add $70 to include $3 million Professional Liability Coverage ... $ _____
☐ Copy of policy, $10 (administrative cost for the 40-page master policy) .... $ _____
☐ Fax service, $10 (Certificate of Insurance faxed to you) FAX#: _____ $ _____
☐ Next Day Air, $30 (requires street address for delivery) .... $ _____
☐ Certificate Holder/Additional Insured, $10 each (please complete reverse side of this form) ... $ _____
☐ Please post my company name on the Internet, $10: _____ $ _____
☐ Please post my techniques on the Internet, $10 for 1 to 3 techniques, $20 for 4 to 7 techniques $ _____
  (1)_____ (2)_____ (3)_____ (4)_____
  (5)_____ (6)_____ (7)_____
  Total $ _____

Method of payment: ☐ Check# _____ Payable to IMA ☐ Money Order# _____ Payable to IMA ☐ Visa ☐ MasterCard ☐ AMEX ☐ Discover

PRINT NAME ON CARD _____ CARDHOLDER'S ZIP CODE _____

Card# ☐☐☐☐ ☐☐☐☐ ☐☐☐☐ ☐☐☐☐ Exp. Date ☐☐ ☐☐

CARDHOLDER'S SIGNATURE _____ DATE _____

Printed: 9/01

The Business of Yoga

Insurance Program For Yoga Teachers & Studios

A comprehensive insurance package to suit your individual needs and give you peace of mind. Discounts on *Yoga Journal* sponsored products, magazine subscriptions, and the support of the CYTA community in teaching yoga. CYTA represents teachers and yoga studios throughout the U.S.

Protect yourself with insurance coverage for you or your studio - as low as $175 - Call 800-395-8075

- General and Professional Liability
- Personal Liability
- Among the industry's lowest rates and flexible policies for special needs such as onsite events
- A-rated insurance company
- 50 states and U.S. Territories
- Discounted coverage
- Special rates for part-time instructors

Your CYTA membership costs $50 (group membership $95) and includes these:
- One Yoga Journal subscription (two for group members)
- 10% off Yoga Journal "Shop YJ" orders
- 10% off a logo listing in Yoga Journal's Teachers Directory
- Entitled to free listing on website

Please see CYTA code of Professional Standards @ yogateachersassoc.org

Our insurance agent, Fitness & Wellness Insurance Agency, Frank Murria & Frick, offers friendly service. We presently write insurance for over 1000 teachers. Visa and Mastercard accepted. CA Lic # OB28716

CYTA Insurance Program of Murria & Frick Insurance Agency, Inc.
800-395-8075 • FAX 858-513-XXXX • murria@murriafrick.com • yogateachersassoc.org

JULY/AUGUST 2003   YOGA JOURNAL 113

5.) Licenses, Permits, & Other Paperwork

(The Lord's Prayer contains 56 words. Lincoln's Gettysburg Address, 268 words. The Declaration of Independence, 1,322 words. Federal regulations governing the sale of cabbage, 26,911 words. –from <u>Small Time Operator</u>)

While most of us would prefer that government bureaucracies disappear into the night, *<u>we ignore them at our peril</u>*. Every government agency seems to want a piece of each and every business, mostly (it seems) to collect fees. As a yoga teacher, the forms should be minimal. In fact, there may be none at all. But requirements vary from region to region, and are changing all the time, so you have to ask. **An easy place to check up on what you may need is at your County Clerk's office.** As with any government office, try to visit at a slow time of the day and week, when the clerks are more relaxed and helpful (don't expect long conversations during the lunch hour.) Explain what you are doing (this can be done anonymously by phone if you prefer) and ask what is required by the county. It may be nothing, or nothing more than a fictitious name (Doing Business As) form. Ask about city, state, and federal regulations while you're at it, or get contact numbers for that information. Though it is unlikely as a solo yoga teacher, you may need a local business license. It's always a good idea to check these things out. It costs you nothing and it's worth the peace of mind.

If you are renting or leasing space we will discuss all that in Part IV.

If you are planning to teach classes out of your home or do any kind of business from your residence , check the zoning laws for your area. Some types of businesses may be permitted and while others are not. Often how you conduct your home-based business is equally important. Always be sensitive to neighborhood needs and concerns. If you are considerate about your class hours and sensitive to parking issues, you are less likely to run into neighborhood problems.

If you go into business by any other name than your own, you should file a DBA (Doing Business As) form, also known as a Fictitious Business form. You will have to file the form (See the example that follows) with your County Clerk's office, and publish your intent in a local newspaper. This accomplishes two things, besides costing you money. It prevents other businesses from using your name, and it lets the public know who's behind the business name you are using. You will have to renew this periodically, and cancel it if you go out of business. You will need to take a copy of this form to your bank if you plan on opening a bank account using the DBA name.

As you can see with the sample DBA/Fictitious Business Form that follows, most forms are simple enough; just write clearly and pay your money.

Another checklist question:

Have I submitted all the necessary forms for my business to the appropriate agencies?

Filing/Renewal

Fictitious Business Name Statement

1. Complete the filing form. Detailed instructions are included on the reverse side of the form. Note that the form requires a **street address**. Post Office boxes are **NOT ACCEPTABLE.**

2. **If filing by mail** or over the counter in Santa Maria or Lompoc, **include a stamped, self-addressed envelope** and either mail your statement to Santa Barbara, or take it back to Santa Maria or Lompoc to be shuttled to Santa Barbara. Filing fees in Santa Maria and Lompoc must be paid by check or money order—the Clerk-Recorder cannot be responsible for filings paid with cash in these offices.

3. The **filing fee** for a Fictitious Business Name Statement is **$27** for one (1) business name and one (1) registrant/owner. Each additional name or registrant costs $5.

4. After filing, you will receive *three* filed copies of the statement from the Santa Barbara office: one is for the **newspaper**, one is for your **bank**, and one is for **your records**. You will also be given a list of adjudicated newspapers in our county and publishing instructions.

Office of KENNETH A. PETTIT
Santa Barbara County Clerk-Recorder-Assessor
P. O. Box 159, Santa Barbara, Ca. 93102

Santa Barbara: (805) 568-2250   Santa Maria: (805) 346-8370
Lompoc: (805) 737-7705

The Business of Yoga

REMINDER

SEE REVERSE SIDE FOR INSTRUCTIONS

✓ $27.00 FILING FEE PAYABLE TO: COUNTY CLERK-RECORDER-ASSESSOR.
✓ $5.00 FOR EACH ADDITIONAL FICTITIOUS BUSINESS NAME AND REGISTRANT'S NAME FILED ON THE SAME STATEMENT AND DOING BUSINESS AT THE SAME LOCATION.
✓ PROVIDE RETURN SELF-ADDRESSED STAMPED ENVELOPE, IF MAILED.
✓ AN ADDENDUM FORM IS AVAILABLE FOR ADDITIONAL BUSINESS & REGISTRANTS' NAMES. IS ADDENDUM ATTACHED? ☐ YES ☐ NO Total number of pages attached:

FICTITIOUS BUSINESS NAME STATEMENT

THE FOLLOWING PERSON(S) IS (ARE) DOING BUSINESS AS:

1a. FICTITIOUS BUSINESS NAME(S) (limit of 6 fictitious business names per statement)

2. STREET ADDRESS, CITY & STATE OF PRINCIPAL PLACE OF BUSINESS IN CALIFORNIA ZIP CODE

3. FULL NAME OF REGISTRANT (IF CORPORATION - SHOW STATE OF INCORPORATION)

RESIDENCE ADDRESS CITY STATE ZIP CODE

FULL NAME OF REGISTRANT (IF CORPORATION - SHOW STATE OF INCORPORATION)

RESIDENCE ADDRESS CITY STATE ZIP CODE

FULL NAME OF REGISTRANT (IF CORPORATION - SHOW STATE OF INCORPORATION)

RESIDENCE ADDRESS CITY STATE ZIP CODE

4. THIS BUSINESS IS CONDUCTED BY: (CHECK ONE ONLY)
☐ AN INDIVIDUAL ☐ A GENERAL PARTNERSHIP ☐ A LIMITED PARTNERSHIP ☐ A BUSINESS TRUST
☐ A CORPORATION ☐ AN UNINCORPORATED ASSOCIATION OTHER THAN A PARTNERSHIP ☐ COPARTNERS
☐ HUSBAND & WIFE ☐ JOINT VENTURE ☐ LIMITED LIABILITY COMPANY ☐ LIMITED LIABILITY PARTNERSHIP
OTHER - PLEASE SPECIFY

5. SIGN BELOW

SIGNED
TYPE OR PRINT NAME HERE

IF REGISTRANT IS A CORPORATION OR LIMITED LIABILITY COMPANY, SIGN BELOW
CORPORATION NAME
SIGNATURE & TITLE
TYPE OR PRINT NAME HERE

THIS STATEMENT WAS FILED WITH THE COUNTY CLERK OF SANTA BARBARA COUNTY OF DATE INDICATED BY FILE STAMP ABOVE.

6. ☐ FIRST FILING ☐ RENEWAL FILING, Current File No.

7. THE REGISTRANT COMMENCED TO TRANSACT BUSINESS ON:

©Astraea Corp. 2005 pg. 85

6.) Pricing; What to Charge and How to Determine It

(Too many people know the price of everything, but not the value.)

Pricing your services is easier than it seems once you remove a lot of the emotional issues. Once you are teaching, you will be given a lot of the information you need. As you fill in at various studios and start to become part of the yoga teaching community, you will find out from other teachers what to charge for classes and private sessions, and what beginning teachers are getting paid in your area. You can also get this information from flyers, ads, and schedules. Generally, the marketplace will not only give you its permission to teach yoga, but will set your price as well. If a well-respected teacher with twenty years of experience is charging $120 an hour for a private lesson, a beginning teacher is more likely to get $50-$60 per hour than $150 per hour.

If you are trying to start a new program at an athletic club, senior center, or local business, pricing is a bit more complicated. To get them interested you may need to give a free lecture, demonstration, or even a class — but this is a marketing tool, to get them educated and excited about you and about yoga. Before you set a price, find out what your sponsor needs for renting the space, if anything, and factor that in. Try to get people to sign up for a series of classes and offer a discount if they prepay. Set a minimum number for each class so you don't end up committed to teaching two students for six weeks of classes. Don't undercharge for your services. It is often said that people don't appreciate a product or service unless they pay up for it. But be careful. While this may be true, if you overcharge for your services you will price yourself right out of the market. Again, once you start teaching and talking with peers, you'll get a sense of what is appropriate.

As far as hard numbers go, in my area $50-$60 for an hour private yoga session and $10-$15 per student for classes (that's what a studio will charge, as a teacher at that studio — you'll get less) seem to be the going rates for new instructors. With private sessions, always insist on a 24-hour cancellation policy. Put it in the release, waiver, or contract that each of your private clients signs and make it stick.

7.) Marketing: Finding Students and Having Students Find You

(Find a need and fill it! (Written on a cement truck) from *Small Time Operator*)

What you spend on marketing is up to you and your budget. Whatever you do, keep track of what generates business and what doesn't. (If you don't get any leads from the lecture you gave at the Chamber of Commerce breakfast, you might not want to go back.) A simple and cheap way to track marketing results is to ask your students how they found you. Consider building the question into your class sign-in sheets or release forms.

You will find that there are many different ways to get your name out into the community, and many of them require little or no money--just imagination and your time. Remember that your marketing is really all about introducing you and your teaching to potential students and clients.

Think about where and how you want to teach and target those places first. While you might not get hired at these places immediately, they will at least know that you are interested, even if there are no openings at the moment. Check back with your contact at each location periodically, to make sure that your name is still in front of them and they know you are still interested and available. Don't phone every day. Be persistent, but don't be a pest.

If you don't like the terms "marketing or advertising," think of it as educating the community about you and your services. In fact, giving free lectures or demonstrations and volunteering at community events are great ways to market your services, and they cost nothing but your time. Try different approaches. I suspect that any place where people gather has the potential to offer yoga classes—churches, schools, businesses, clubs, and so on. The local college may need yoga instructors. What about Adult Education evening programs?

Whenever you are driving, have an active eye and an open mind. Ask yourself: "Could that place use a yoga instructor? How about that business? Would that be a good building for a yoga studio?"

If you are already involved in your community, you've got a good start. If a friend runs a neighborhood athletic club, if an old high school teacher volunteers at Girls Inc., talk with them about a yoga program. Talk about your teacher training experience with friends and teachers at your yoga studio. **Networking can sound so clinical and "yuppie," but so often "business" comes out of conversation**. If people know you already, they may be positive and supportive about your new profession in yoga.

If you have no contacts or friends (we'll assume you've moved to a new town, and that you are not a horrible, unfriendly person), take yoga classes everywhere you can and get involved with community activities and organizations that are of interest to you. If you have to resort to cold-calling companies and organizations, find out something about them first: what they do, what civic activities or charities they support, how they take care of their employees, and, if possible, a contact person (maybe the human resources director, or activities director). I personally think 'cold calling' is ineffective at best, but with a bit of background information and a contact (let's call this luke-warm calling), you will certainly have a better chance.

If you end up teaching at a location other than a yoga studio, or a private home, it is best to have a simple written agreement. Whether it's at a Girl's Club, a church or a large business, a written agreement that lays out each party's responsibilities should be signed well before you begin that first class. The agreement needs to be dated and signed (by both parties) and include: fees, how & when you will get paid, liability (they may want to see proof of insurance), the responsibilities of each party, and a cancellation policy. Once you have done these a few times, develop a standard form. It will save you time, effort and money.

Here is a general list of what should be in a contract (although you might not need all of these to rent the local church's game room):

- **Names and addresses of the parties**
- **Date the contract is signed**
- **A short background of the agreement**
- **What each party is promising to do**
- **When the work or service will be done or provided**
- **How long the contract will remain in effect**
- **The fee for your services**
- **When the payment is due**
- **Warranties or guarantees**
- **Termination conditions**
- **Are rights transferable?**
- **Arbitration or mediation of disputes**

Take a look at the sample contract that follows.

Another Business Planning Checklist Question:

Do I have a standardized contract for teaching at business and community locations?

Ashley Walker – Yoga Instructor

1245 Seagull Lane
Bodega Bay, Ca. 94555
Ph. 707-555-5555

<u>**An Agreement between:**</u>
Ashley Walker – Yoga Instructor and   <u>Bodega Bay Girls Inc.</u>

This agreement between Ashley Walker and Bodega Bay Girls Inc. (located at 120 Main St., Bodega Bay, Ca.) outlines the details for yoga classes that will be offered by Ashley Walker at the Girls Inc. facility on Main St. in Bodega Bay.

<u>Time & Place</u>: Ashley Walker will teach classes once a week on Monday nights at 7:30 pm in the main room. The classes will be one hour in length, but the room will be kept available between 7:15 pm and 9:00pm. The classes will run for all of 2003.

<u>**Fees & Payment:**</u> **Ashley Walker will be paid $80 per class, and will teach a maximum of 12 students (due to space constraints) and a minimum of two students. Girls Inc. will pay her monthly. Ashley Walker will not be charged for the use of the space.**

<u>Liability</u>: Girls Inc. carries and will maintain a master policy that covers outside activities such as this for damage, injury and liability. Ashley Walker carries and will maintain liability insurance for teaching classes of up to 99 students during the term of this agreement. Copies of both policies are available on demand.

<u>Responsibilities:</u>   Girls Inc. will be responsible for making sure the room is cleared by 7:15 each Monday night and making sure that the temperature in the room is at least 74 degrees. Ashley Walker is responsible for preparing and organizing the classes and providing any equipment she may need, other than the students' personal yoga mats. She is also responsible for leaving the room as she found it.

<u>Cancellation Policy</u>: Girls Inc. agrees to give Ashley Walker a minimum of 24 hours notice prior to canceling a scheduled class, or agrees to pay in full for that class. Ashley Walker agrees to provide the same notice or forfeit fees. She may, at her discretion, hire a qualified and insured yoga instructor to take her place, in the event of illness or other irregular and unavoidable absences.

<u>Terms:</u> Changes to the terms can be made by the mutual consent of both parties. Either party can cancel this business relationship with thirty days notice.

_____ _____   _____ _____
Ashley Walker   Date   For Bodega Bay Girls, Inc.   Date

FLYERS- **One popular and effective way of getting your name out there, especially once you have some classes set up, is the single page flyer.** These are a relatively inexpensive way of advertising you and your classes. If you are handy with a computer and a digital camera you can create one yourself. If you have a graphic artist friend or student, maybe a trade can be arranged. I've found that professionally done flyers cost on average about $200 dollars for the artwork. Once you have a basic format, it will be cheap and easy to change dates and locations for future offerings. And of course, copies can be made in large or small quantities, as needed, at your local copy shop.

Be imaginative with your flyer. Make it different. **When you are starting out and have more time than money, don't be afraid to offer free classes. Offer coupons for free classes, if you have unused space in your class.** Having students take your class is about the best advertising you can do. Also, in flyers and in all advertising consider offering discounts for a series of classes, if the students prepay. These always work to your advantage. Consider putting coupons in flyers or print ads that offer discounts or allow a friend in for free.

Several flyers follow this page. Don't be afraid to copy ideas that you like, but again you want your own distinctive ads. Remember, **yoga is getting more and more popular, which means more and more competition for you as a teacher**. Differentiate yourself from the pack.

The Business of Yoga

Forrest Yoga Workshop with Heather Tiddens

April 30 – May 2, 2004

Gravity Surfing: Inversions and Arm Balancing Asanas

- Levels 2/3, 3
- Cost: $125
- Bring two mats, a towel and a strap.
- Room will be heated to 80°. Come prepared to sweat and go deep!

SANTA BARBARA YOGA CENTER
32 E. Micheltorena St.
Santa Barbara, CA 93101
(805)965-6045
www.SantaBarbaraYogaCenter.com

Payments for workshops are non-refundable, but may be converted into credit (minus $10 processing fee) if cancellation is made with a minimum of 48-hour notice.

Fri. 4/30 6:30pm - 8:30pm, Sat. 5/1 1:00pm - 4:00pm, Sun. 5/2 1:00pm - 4:00pm

Take flight! Inversions and arm balancing asanas are challenging, thrilling, and very rejuvenating for the mind and body. Learn step by step the fundamentals of lift-off, moving through the air with grace, and landing with precision and lightness. From learning the basic stages of Handstand and Shoulderstand, to discovering the more advanced arm balances, Heather will guide you through Forrest Yoga asanas that build core awareness, strength, and space in your practice. As you connect your lines of energy from your core through your legs and arms, "surfing" gravity becomes accessible and fun. Learn to go beyond your habitual quit points in these poses and transform your relationship to gravity. *(Note: This workshop may not be suitable for people with heart problems, detached retinas, ear problems, wrist or arm injuries, or for women who are pregnant.)*

Heather Tiddens: Heather teaches yoga as a tool for helping students become their most genuine selves. Her classes are known for their physical intensity and detailed instruction, as well as being a safe, sacred space for students to explore their spiritual, emotional and physical healing and growth. Her teaching is inspired by her own healing process which integrates Forrest Yoga, hands-on healing, psychotherapy, and Native American ceremony and shamanism. Heather's life-long athletic experience and deep connection with the elements of nature influence her work greatly. Since 1979, she has been an avid and skilled surfer, competing as one of the top 15 women on the Professional World Tour in 1988-89. Heather has studied and been certified in various styles of hatha yoga, and since 1998, she has worked extensively with Ana Forrest as her student, apprentice, and assistant in workshops and Forrest Yoga Teacher Trainings throughout the country. Heather is based in Santa Barbara, CA, where she teaches at the Santa Barbara Yoga Center, and at Satya House, her private studio. She teaches the Introduction to Yoga Program and Teacher's Tutorial at the SBYC, as well as ongoing beginning, intermediate, and advanced level classes, courses and workshops.

Forrest Yoga: Ana Forrest has spent 30 years developing Forrest Yoga specifically to address Our People's stresses and challenges, both physical and emotional. We use heat, deep breathing and intense pose sequences, compassionately taught, to develop skills in awakening each of the senses. You will learn to bring aliveness into every cell of your physical body, as well as exercising your emotional body through the full spectrum of feeling; from the healing process all the way into the ecstatic realms. Forrest Yoga challenges you to heal, grow, and welcome your spirit home.

The Business of Yoga

Siddhi's Summer Yogi Cleanse

When the moon is waning it is easier to let go!

An 11-Day Cleanse to: Tonify, Detoxify & Balance Your Body, Mind & Spirit

- Strenghten, Revitalize & Purify Your Entire Body
- Improve Your Digestion And Elimination
- Regenerate & Restore Your Vital Energy
- Free Your Mind & Balance Your Emotions
- Transform & Uplift Your Spirit
- Increase Your Awareness, Inner Power & Self-Confidence

Daily Kundalini Yoga classes from 7:00-8:30 AM to detox and vitalize your Liver, Colon, Stomach, Digestion, Elimination, your Nervous System and your Circulation, as well as bring into balance your Blood and the Non-Physical Bodies.

SANTA BARBARA YOGA CENTER
www.SantaBarbaraYogaCenter.com
32 East Micheltorena Street
Tel: 805.965.6045

Wednesday, July 31 through Saturday, August 10, 2002
(Pre-registration is required for product ordering by 7/20)

$235 (Classes & Cleansing Products)

The Business of Yoga

Afro-Brazilian Dance
with Vanessa Isaac

Come join Vanessa's soulful celebration of music and dance in one of the most popular classes in town, now at the Santa Barbara Yoga Center.

Vanessa mixes Brazilian, Afro and movement awareness in a class full of fun.

"Vanessa's success as a teacher has a lot to do with her warmth, charm and knack for making people feel at ease, but it's her skill and knowledge that truly brings her students an authentic experience."
— The S. B. Independent

Sundays, 4:30-5:30pm
Begins June 9, 2002

Single class $12
Series of 4 classes $40 (to be used within 60 days)

SANTA BARBARA YOGA CENTER
www.SantaBarbaraYogaCenter.com
32 East Micheltorena Street
805.965.6045

PRINT ADS - If you have a class schedule or rent a space to hold classes, some form of print advertising may be worthwhile. Again, you may have to bear the costs of a graphic artist to create the initial ad.

Look for alternative newspapers or newspapers that your potential students might read. In Santa Barbara, where I live, the alternative paper is called the Independent and enjoys a huge readership. I was surprised to find out how inexpensive ads in that paper are. A quarter page ad costs between three and four dollars a week, depending on how long you run the ad. That would fit almost every small-business ad budget.

A couple of different print ads follow.

The Business of Yoga

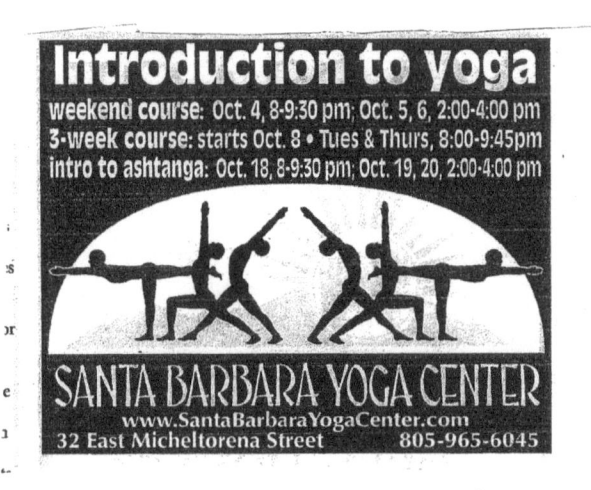

The Business of Yoga

Prayer of Forgiveness

I bless this day and give thanks for my life
I forgive completely all people who have hurt me (3x)
I ask all people I have hurt to please forgive me (3x)
I apologize to myself for my wrongs to myself and my wrongs to others (3x)
I apologize for all my hurts or wrongs to all Life Forms (3x)
With this release, freedom, Peace, power, and new life, I bless
all creation in the entire universe and I fill the entire universe with my love
I love and bless the earth, all life, and all humanity
I love, bless and respect the visible and the invisible
I rejoice and give thanks for my new life, power and health and
give complete blessing and love to all life, always.
—Repeat throughout the day.

Upcoming Events:

At East Beach Studios - Friday, October 11
Before you Hit the bars:
Chanting, Chi Gong & Yoga with Steve Ross (www.steveross.com)
Special Class time 6 p.m. • Chanting at 8pm

At the Yoga Studio - Saturday November 2
Teacher Training with Eddie Ellner Noon — 5 p.m.
Come prepared to learn nothing.
Call 962-2234 for details.

YOGA soup
EAT YOUR HEART OPEN

CLASS SCHEDULE

At East Beach Studio: 201 S. Milpas
Tue/Thu 6:30 p.m.
Fri 7:00 p.m.
Sun 8:30 a.m. & 5:30 p.m.

At Yoga Studio: 1911 De La Vina #G
Mon/Wed 5:45 p.m.

YOGA SOUP • 805-452-9873 • eddie@yogasoup.com • www.yogasoup.com

WEB SITES - I would suggest the same methods for Web sites as we talked about for flyers, although for beginning teachers, I would question the value of Web sites. Again, if you love playing on computers and are adept at it—well, go for it. There is a variety of services and Internet software, some free or at very reasonable prices, that can help you register a domain name, host your Web page, and design a Web page. There are a lot of Web page designers around (many with time on their hands), and you may be able to find one who is willing to barter or at a bargain price.

Whether you need a Web page or not is a question worth thinking about. While it is true that more and more people use the Internet, a Web site for a solo teacher might not be time and cost effective. One way or another, you will spend a fair bit of time and money to get it up and running. You will want it to be sharp, eye-catching, simple and easy to navigate. You will also have to maintain it, and fulfill any offerings you put on it. (This might simply be returning e-mail.) You will need to spend more money if you want to get it advertised on search engines or larger Web sites. All this may be more than you want or are able to do. And **a poorly maintained Web site and unreturned e-mail queries reflect poorly on you.** It may be that as a solo teacher, you are better off distributing your small amount of necessary information by word of mouth, flyers and business cards. And again, your reputation will grow as people get to know you and what you have to offer.

On the other hand, if you are opening a small studio and have lots of information, schedules, teacher resumes, and other information to convey, a site may be worthwhile. But remember the Web site represents you, and if people are turned off by a Web site that is not maintained and unimaginative, they might lose interest and not come back.

There are a lot of Web resources on the net, and they are constantly changing and expanding. Here are a few that may help get you started. If you are going to have a Web site, you'll need to register a domain name first. This is your name or the name you choose for your business. Registering it reserves the name for your use on the Internet. (If you know you will want a Web site at some point, you can register it and reserve it now.)

A Web-designer friend feels that everyone should reserve his or her own name on the Internet. His reasoning is that you don't want someone else using your name on the Internet (perhaps without your knowledge). Further, it might be a good idea to reserve it for some (at this point unknown) future use. There are many sites available to register your domain name. If you can use your company name or your personal name, do so. But in any case keep it simple. You can also set up your e-mail through these sites. There are a number of Internet sites that will help you register your domain name: Budget Register (**http:/www.budgetnic.com**) is a good place to start. Registering will cost about $15 a year. Ask around, there are always new sites that offer competitive pricing.

Once you have your name, you will need a Web-host to host your web page. Your own Internet provider may offer Web-hosting services so that is a good place to start. Server 101 (**http:/www.server101.com**) and Verio (**http:/www.verio.com**) are two other sources. There are a lot of choices, so look around. Check on price (start-up fees and monthly fees) and features (the ability to add and revise items on your Webpage.) Monthly fees vary.

To build your Web page you will need software, which is often available from Web-hosting companies (like Verio), software companies (try Microsoft Frontpage), or your browser (Netscape Communicator.) Most are relatively user friendly; but patience and persistence are required.

Your other choice is to go with a Web designer. If you get help, have definite ideas of what you want done before you meet. The easiest way to find a Web designer in your town is by referral. Ask at your yoga studio, or other businesses in town that have Web sites that you like. Get a few names, get examples of their work, and compare product and price.

Check out the following Web sites and see what you like and what you don't.

www.forrestyoga.com
www.heathertiddensyoga.com
www.sbyoga.com

Another Checklist Question:

What will best suit my marketing needs? Do I need a Web site?

8.) Ten Key Elements to Successful Marketing

(Marketing is educating.)

I. Reputation is everything. If people are happy with your services, they will come back, and they'll tell their friends. If they are unhappy, they'll just tell their friends.

II. Don't confuse marketing with advertising.

III. Marketing is all about educating your clients about your services.

IV. Decide who your target audience is first, <u>and then</u> decide on the right marketing approach.

V. Remember that there are lots of free ways to advertise. Don't be afraid to offer free classes or discounts to get students into the classroom, especially when your classes are not full.

VI. You are your own best advertisement. Offer free demonstrations, classes and lectures at a variety of venues.

VII. Marketing dollars are wasted if they don't bring in business.

VIII. Think about print ads in alternative/independent newspapers. These ads are affordable and will probably reach your target audience.

IX. Considering prepayments and discounts on a series of classes, as a way to bring in new students.

X. Track the success of your marketing by questioning your students or by surveys. Find out what works and what doesn't.

PART II WORKSHOP

In this workshop you will work on developing a marketing program for you and your business. Spend the first part of this workshop writing down five untapped areas of opportunity for teaching yoga in your community. Rank them in order starting with the most promising one.

Next, develop marketing strategies for those five opportunities. Include the best way to approach each situation: lecture, print ad, flyer, etc. Be specific. Feel free to refer to any material in the manual.

Don't take the easy way out. Try to think of unique markets and methods, ones that will help you compete, not just make you another one of the many yoga instructors in your town.

PART II WORKSHOP

PART II WORKSHOP

PART III

1.) What is Bookkeeping? Why Keep a Set of Books?

(The best memory is not so firm as faded ink – Chinese proverb – from Small Time Operator)

For many years, my own experience with accounting and bookkeeping was one of either complete disinterest or stifling boredom. Accounting seemed made for 'bean counters,' and accounting classes were a sure way to catch up on the sleep you missed from partying too hard the night before. In short, accounting and bookkeeping were pretty low on my list. That changed when I started investing, evaluating businesses, and figuring out why some businesses were successful and others were not. Slowly, revenue and sales figures, profit and loss statements, net profit margins became interesting pieces of a puzzle--information that could not only help understand businesses, but guide them.

Many people new to small business think that keeping a set of books is something they do because they have to, a loathesome task. However, there are very good reasons for doing so. Among other things, the IRS requires it. But more importantly, keeping an accurate and up-to-date set of books will provide you with vital information about the health of your business. They can at once act as a thermometer and a barometer of your business. **A business's books can be simple (hand-written in a wire-spined notebook) or complex (General Electric's), but they all share a common purpose: to give the owner(s)** *timely* **and** *complete* **information about their business.**

While most people have good memories (especially in business where their livelihood depends on what comes in and goes out), and business owners develop a general (almost instinctual) idea of how their business is doing, it's almost impossible to recall everything or see how all the moving parts fit together. General ledgers, profit and loss statements, balance sheets--all the things we collectively call 'the books'--give you that complete picture. Like a household budget, they tell you whether more money is going out than coming in, or the reverse, and how much is left. Bookkeeping can be incredibly complex, but it can also be fairly simple—especially for someone whose business is just teaching yoga. **Either way, the goal is to record the information in a way that is understandable and immediately useful to you; otherwise it is a waste of time and effort.**

2.) What You Need to Get Going

(Where are we going, and why am I in this hand-basket - Bumper Sticker)

My purpose here is to give you an introduction to simple bookkeeping and to get your small business running. As you grow larger, and particularly if you open your own studio, you will need an accountant. Not only can he help you prepare your taxes (and keep you current on tax law and deductions), he can also help organize your bookkeeping in a way that is most efficient for your business, and in a way that makes his job both easier and cheaper. <u>You will find that a good accountant, one that you can trust and confide in, will be one of your best business assets.</u>

<u>If your business is anything more than teaching yoga part time, consider finding an accountant</u>. Again, ask friends and colleagues. Don't be afraid to interview different accountants and firms. As with taking on a partner, it is important to find an accountant that you like and trust. Make sure he is comfortable working with you, and you with him. In an interview, you might ask him questions similar to these:

- Do you work with businesses similar to mine?
- Is your firm the right size for my business, and mine for yours?
- Are you willing to be an informal advisor for my business?
- Do you have a sterling record?
- Will you represent me in a tax audit?
- What will your services (accounting & advising) cost?
- (Are we comfortable with each other?)

Let's assume, for the moment, that after teacher training you will start your yoga career in a manner similar to our Ashley Walker example.   That is, you're not opening a studio or renting space, but just want to start teaching. You are serious about building a business teaching yoga and want to set it up right.

<u>Shoebox Accounting</u> - Whether you know it or not, the day you get that first check for filling in at your local yoga studio, you are keeping 'books'. Perhaps later that day, you pick up a set of business cards from the copy shop, drop them and some resumes by a few other studios, and finally fill up your gas tank on the way home.

At the end of the day you stuff the check stub and the expense receipts in a shoebox.

Your business is off and running, and so are your books (the shoebox). Presumably at some point you'll want to cash the check, and others as they come in. But you can keep the shoebox style of bookkeeping going indefinitely and many people do.

I have a friend who is a high-powered and well-compensated attorney. She loves her work, but has no clue about her personal finances (she's always working—and makes a lot of money-- so it doesn't matter). She finds out about her personal finances once a year. A little before tax time (she always gets an extension), she gets her boxes that she has thrown her bills, pay stubs, credit card receipts, etc. into throughout the year, and dumps them off at her accountant's office. He sorts through it all (at large expense), figures out her taxes, and gives her a financial picture for the last year. I've seen some businesses run this way too. It can work for a while, but usually not for long. **A better way is to develop a system that keeps you up-to-date on revenues (what you take in), expenses (what goes out), and cash balances (what's left) -- from the beginning. As a sole proprietor (meaning that you are the only one in the business), this system is easy to set up.**

The Business Bank Account -A first step is to isolate business-related income and expenses from all your other financial dealings. A simple and inexpensive way to accomplish this is to setup a separate bank account (look for free checking, it is still offered at some banks), and run every business item through that checking account. If you have a fictitious business name, use that, and don't forget to take a copy of the filed form with you when you open the account. Draw cash from that account for incidental business expenses, and if you get a business credit card, use it only for business expenses and pay its bill from your business account. Record everything, and if you take money out to live on, record that as well—as a person withdrawal or 'draw.' The idea is that only business-related items come and go from this account. Try to keep it that way, and take care of personal business in your personal checking account. **The business banking account then becomes a sort of general ledger for your business. A separate bank account for your business is an important first step in getting your business books in order.**

(Incidentally, computer programs like Quicken allow you to categorize all items going in and out of single and multiple checking accounts. This is a big help if business expenses come out of a personal account or vice-a-versa. We'll take a brief look at Quicken programs later on.)

Another Checklist Question:
Have I set up a checking account for my new business?

3.) Simple Ledgers

("Make everything as simple as possible, but not simpler.") - Albert Einstein)

Ledgers have been around, in one form or another, as long as there have been business transactions, barters, and trades. A ledger is a record of financial transactions. **For our purposes here, and for your purposes in opening a small business, we will be talking about "cash accounting" (vs. accrual) and single entry (vs. double entry) ledgers.**

Business ledgers help track and categorize different expense and income items over time. (Your business checking account statement, while it may have this information in it, doesn't organize the items in a useful way, as a ledger does.)

A good ledger will tell you lots of things about your business: the business had income of $3,000 for the year and expenses of $5,000 (Oops!); utilities are running $1,000 per month for my 900 sq. ft space (Yikes! Do I have a water leak, should I turn down the heat?); my tab at the restaurant downstairs for July was twice what it was in June (Burp! Was that the same month my brother-in-law was in town?).

Ledgers provide a revealing and useful look at your business. You might see that revenues (class numbers increased) went up in July, the same month you posted flyers out at the university. They might show that your income dropped below your expenses when you were sick for two weeks in March. You might notice that auto expenses for 2002 were three times what they were in 2001 (your car was in the shop a lot), and that cut into profits for 2002. Is it time to get a new car?

The latter example brings up a key point about ledgers: they should not be viewed in isolation. **Numbers work best *for you* when they are compared.** How did your business do this year compared to last year? Did it grow? Maybe you took in more money this year than last, but spent more too? What happened to profits—the famous 'bottom line?' Comparing similar income and expense categories over time can help you improve efficiencies and profits in your business, and tell you where and how to grow your business.

4.) Some Simple Bookkeeping Terminology

("Half this game is ninety percent mental." - Yogi Berra)

This list of terms and the sample ledgers that follow should help get you started. Several good sources for ledgers, financial statements, and financial reports are also listed in the Book and Resource Guide in the back of your manual. **You will be amazed at your interest in these terms and numbers, once they relate to your own business and your own paycheck.**

Revenue, Sales, or Income - This is the so-called "Top-line" (it's always at the top of Income and Profit & Loss Statements). It is what a business takes in for its products or services (your check for teaching a yoga class, or the coffee shop's sale of a breakfast). I like the term revenue best because it is most exact. You don't record a sale when you teach a yoga class. Income in the corporate world could be: gross income, operating income, pre-tax income, or net income. This top line is best called revenue or gross income.

Non-Business, Miscellaneous or Other Income – This is incidental income that comes into your business. It is not related to the business's primary purpose. Your main revenue comes from teaching yoga. If you buy and then return some equipment, the return credit would come under miscellaneous income, and offset the expense. It is important to keep such items separate. It is also important to determine what income is taxable and what is not, and record it as such.

Expenses (Expenditures) - These would include all payments including cash outlays related to the business. It is important to keep track of all expenses in a business and to categorize them into groups. This helps provide the best picture of where your expense dollars are going. Also, many business expenses are tax deductible and can help reduce your tax bill.

Pre-tax Income- This is what's left after you deduct all your business expenses from the revenue and other income, but before you pay taxes.

Assets – These are anything of value that is owned by your business. Cash assets are just that, the amount of cash that the business has in its accounts. Accounts receivable is the money owed to your business; for example you may have taught and billed a client but the money has not yet been received. These count as assets as well. If you have a business that requires keeping an inventory of products, those count as well. Other assets might be your phone, car, or equipment that you own and have on hand for students. **Whatever they are, business assets must be wholly owned by the business.**

Liabilities (Debt) – This is what your business owes. For a solo yoga teacher, this might simply be debt on a business credit card (for the computer you bought to help with the bookkeeping). Accounts payable, that is, the monthly bills you pay, count as debt, if they are outstanding and due (hence – payable).

Balance Sheet – A balance sheet (like a personal net worth statement) lists all of the business's assets and liabilities *at a specific point in time* (typically at the end of the year). Subtracting liabilities from assets will give the net worth or equity of the business.

Income Statement (Profit and Loss Statement) - This lists all sources of income and all expenses over a given period of time typically a month, a quarter (3 months), or a year. It compares what you've brought in with what you've spent for that period, and usually gives a net profit or loss (Income-Expenses).

Cash Flow Statement – This tracks the cash that goes in and out of your business over a given period of time.

Cash Flow Projections - Try to predict a business's future cash needs. These can help a small business avoid a sudden cash squeeze or help it get through its early months. It is always important to have enough cash on hand for unusual expenses, or unpredictable revenues. **A cash reserve is a must for small businesses.**

Following this page are simple examples of ledgers for Ashley Walker's solo yoga business. Following those ledgers are an Income Statement, Balance Sheet, and Cash Flow Statement for a golf apparel company with $125 million in annual revenues. Though our simple ledgers for *Ashley Walker – Yoga Instructor* look much different, the structures and concepts are the same.

It is crucial to understand that Ashley Walker's Income, Expense, and Profit and Loss Ledgers are derived from the very first general ledger. All of a business's books are built off a general ledger that records (day in and day out) all business transactions. Note that each transaction in the general ledger is numbered so that it can be identified in the subsequent sheets.

Checklist questions:

Do I understand simple bookkeeping and its terminology?
Can I set up simple ledgers and track income and expenses for my business?

The Business of Yoga

Ashley Walker - Yoga Instructor

General Ledger   Month of   **Sept. 02**

Date		Transaction	Payment Cash/Check	Amount Dollars	Taxable/
9/4/2002	1	Mrs. Griffin (Private)	Cash	60.00	Yes
9/4/2002	2	Chevron/Gas	Cash	(26.75)	
9/09/	3	Girls, Inc.	Check	80.00	Yes
9/10/2002	4	AT&T Wirelss/Cell Phone	Check	(60.25)	
9/11/2002	5	Mrs. Griffin (Private)	Cash	60.00	Yes
9/11/2002	6	Gaiam Cat./Yoga Mats	Check	(73.24)	
9/12/2002	7	Kinko's/Flyers	Check	(14.50)	
9/12/2002	8	Brenda Rogers (Private)	Check	60.00	Yes
9/16/2002	9	Girls Inc.	Check	80.00	Yes
9/16/2002	10	Chevron/Gas	Cash	(18.97)	
9/18/2002	11	Mrs. Griffin (Private)	Cash	60.00	Yes
9/18/2002	12	Jiffy Lube Oil Change*	Cash	(21.20)	
9/19/2002	13	Brenda Rogers (Private)	Check	60.00	Yes
9/19/2002	14	Title 9 Sports/Yoga Tights	Check	(45.54)	
9/23/2002	15	Girls, Inc.	Check	80.00	Yes
9/25/2002	16	Mrs. Griffin (Private)	Cash	60.00	Yes
9/30/2002	17	Girls, Inc.	Check	80.00	Yes
9/30/2002	18	AT&T Wireless/Refund	Check	12.42	

Total Transactions   431.97

*-Only a portion is deductible

Ashley Walker - Yoga Instructor

REVENUE/GR. INCOME LEDGER　　　Month of　　Sept. 02

Date		Client	Payment Cash/Check	Amount Dollars	Taxable/
9/4/2002	1	Mrs. Griffin (Private)	Cash	60.00	Yes
9/9/2002	3	Girls, Inc.	Check	80.00	Yes
9/11/2002	5	Mrs. Griffin (Private)	Cash	60.00	Yes
9/12/2002	8	Brenda Rogers (Private)	Check	60.00	Yes
9/16/2002	9	Girls Inc.	Check	80.00	Yes
9/18/2002	11	Mrs. Griffin (Private)	Cash	60.00	Yes
9/19/2002	13	Brenda Rogers (Private)	Check	60.00	Yes
9/23/2002	15	Girls, Inc.	Check	80.00	Yes
9/25/2002	16	Mrs. Griffin (Private)	Cash	60.00	Yes
9/30/2002	17	Girls, Inc.	Check	80.00	Yes
9/30/2002	18	AT&T Wireless Refund	Check	12.42	No
		Total Gross Income		692.42	

Ashley Walker - Yoga Instructor

Expense Ledger			Month of	Sept. 02
Date		PAYEE/PURPOSE	Payment Cash/Check	Amount Dollars
9/4/2002	2	Chevron/Gas	Cash	26.75
9/10/2002	4	AT&T Wireless/Cellphone	Check	60.25
9/11/2002	6	Gaiam Catalog/Yoga Mats	Check	73.24
9/12/2002	7	Kinko's/ Flyers	Check	14.50
9/16/2002	10	Chevron/Gas	Cash	18.97
9/18/2002	12	Jiffy Lube/Oil Change*	Cash	21.20
9/19/2002	14	Title 9 Sports/Yoga tights	Check	45.54

Total Expenses   260.45

The Business of Yoga

Ashley Walker   Yoga Instructor

Month of   Sept.   02

PROFIT & LOSS LEDGER   Amount

INCOME

Classes (3,9,15,17)	$320.00
Private Instruction (1,5,8,11,13,16)	$360.00
Other (18)	$12.42
TOTAL INCOME	**$692.42**

EXPENSES

Cell Phone (4)	-$60.25
Auto Gas (2,10)	-$45.72
Auto Service* (12)	-$21.20
Yoga Equipment (6)	-$73.24
Yoga Clothing (14)	-$45.54
Marketing/Flyers (7)	-$14.50
TOTAL EXPENSES	**-$260.45**

NET PRE-TAX INCOME   **$431.97**
(Income-Expenses)

The Business of Yoga

Ashley Walker - Yoga Instructor

Cash Flow Projection   Month of   Oct. 02

Date		Cash In	Cash Out	Balance
10/1/2002	Cash on Hand*			3,252.00
	1st Week Income	150.00		
	1st Week Expenses		75.00	
	2nd Week Income	150.00		
	2nd Week Expenses		75.00	
	Auto Brakes		350.00	
	3rd Week Income	-		
	3rd Week Expenses		95.00	
10/23/2002	One Time 3 Hour Private	200.00		
	4th Week Income	150.00		
	4th Week Expenses		75.00	
	Total Cash In	650.00		
	Total Cash Out		670.00	
10/31/2002	Cash on Hand			3,232.00
	* - In Business Checking Account			

The Business of Yoga

	Ashley Walker Financial	Yoga Instructor Projections	
	Year 1	Year 2	Year 3
Income			
Classes	2*48*$30= $2,880	4*48*$60=$11,520	6*48*$100=$28,800
Privates	2*48*$60=$5,760	4*48*85=$16,320	6*48*$90=$25,920
Total Income	$8,640	$27,840	$54,720
Expenses			
Auto	$4,000	$5,000	$6,000
Liability Insurance	$200	$200	$200
Health Insurance	$0	$1500	$1500
Phone	$800	$800	$800
Taxes(@ .20 TI)	$1,728	$5,568	$10,944
Clothing	$1,000	$2,000	$2,500
Advertising	$300	$1,000	$1,500
Equipment	$1,000	$1,000	$1,000
Misc.	$200	$1,000	$1,500
Total Expense	$9,228	$17,868	$25,744
Net Pre-Tax Income	$(588)	$9,972	$28,976

** Note that the expenses are for additional yoga teaching expenses, and not personal expenses. Ashley should take those into account, not necessarily here, but in her overall financial picture.

ASHWORTH, INC. AND SUBSIDIARIES

Consolidated Statements of Income

For the years ended October 31, 2001, 2000 and 1999

	2001	2000	1999
Net revenues	$124,727,000	$125,947,000	$107,921,000
Cost of goods sold	76,448,000	76,963,000	68,558,000
Gross profit	48,279,000	48,984,000	39,363,000
Selling, general and administrative expenses	42,118,000	36,603,000	32,867,000
Income from operations	6,161,000	12,381,000	6,496,000
Other income (expense):			
Interest income	21,000	204,000	112,000
Interest expense	(1,352,000)	(640,000)	(431,000)
Net foreign currency exchange loss	(90,000)	(939,000)	(23,000)
Other income (expense), net	(27,000)	(18,000)	113,000
Total other expense	(1,448,000)	(1,393,000)	(229,000)
Income before provision for income taxes	4,713,000	10,988,000	6,267,000
Provision for income taxes	1,885,000	4,391,000	2,450,000
Net income	$ 2,828,000	$ 6,597,000	$ 3,817,000
Net income per share:			
Basic	.22	.49	.27
Diluted	.21	.49	.27
Weighted-average shares outstanding:			
Basic	13,140,000	13,406,000	14,035,000
Diluted	13,408,000	13,467,000	14,045,000

See accompanying notes to consolidated financial statements.

ASHWORTH, INC. AND SUBSIDIARIES

Consolidated Balance Sheets

October 31, 2001 and 2000

Assets	2001	2000
Current assets:		
Cash and cash equivalents	$ 1,055,000	$ 1,231,000
Accounts receivable – trade, net of allowance for doubtful accounts of $2,141,000 and $1,238,000 in 2001 and 2000, respectively	26,817,000	25,578,000
Accounts receivable – other	2,199,000	2,221,000
Inventories, net	35,841,000	37,526,000
Income tax receivable	941,000	582,000
Other current assets	2,359,000	1,891,000
Deferred income tax asset	1,833,000	1,614,000
Total current assets	71,045,000	70,643,000
Property, plant and equipment, at cost:		
Land	1,200,000	1,200,000
Buildings and improvements	2,889,000	2,818,000
Production equipment	10,314,000	10,065,000
Furniture and equipment	18,014,000	13,639,000
Leasehold improvements	4,090,000	2,730,000
	36,507,000	30,452,000
Less accumulated depreciation and amortization	(17,862,000)	(15,604,000)
	18,645,000	14,848,000
Other assets	3,966,000	1,880,000
Total assets	$93,656,000	$87,371,000

(Continued)

ASHWORTH, INC. AND SUBSIDIARIES

Consolidated Balance Sheets, Continued

October 31, 2001 and 2000

Liabilities and Stockholders' Equity	2001	2000
Current liabilities:		
Line of credit payable	$5,950,000	$1,490,000
Current portion of long-term debt	659,000	692,000
Accounts payable	4,203,000	4,477,000
Accrued liabilities:		
Salaries and commissions	1,675,000	2,272,000
Other	1,631,000	1,716,000
Total current liabilities	14,118,000	10,647,000
Long-term debt, net of current portion	3,166,000	3,293,000
Deferred income tax liability	752,000	742,000
Other long-term liabilities	626,000	715,000
Stockholders' equity:		
Common stock, $.001 par value; authorized 50,000,000 shares; issued and outstanding 13,148,000 and 13,109,000 shares in 2001 and 2000, respectively	13,000	13,000
Capital in excess of par value	37,959,000	37,698,000
Retained earnings	38,069,000	35,241,000
Accumulated other comprehensive loss	(1,047,000)	(978,000)
Total stockholders' equity	74,994,000	71,974,000
Commitments and contingencies		
Total liabilities and stockholders' equity	$93,656,000	$87,371,000

See accompanying notes to consolidated financial statements.

ASHWORTH, INC. AND SUBSIDIARIES

Consolidated Statements of Cash Flows

For the years ended October 31, 2001, 2000 and 1999

	2001	2000	1999
Cash flows from operating activities:			
Net income	$ 2,828,000	$ 6,597,000	$ 3,817,000
Adjustments to reconcile net income to net cash provided by operating activities:			
Amortization of deferred compensation	—	—	8,000
Depreciation and amortization	3,125,000	2,602,000	2,067,000
(Gain) loss on disposal of property, plant and equipment	83,000	(1,000)	11,000
Increase in deferred income tax asset	(209,000)	(119,000)	(5,000)
Provision for doubtful accounts, markdowns and sales returns	1,664,000	744,000	309,000
Increase in accounts receivable	(2,903,000)	(5,663,000)	(2,806,000)
Decrease (increase) in inventories	1,685,000	(6,882,000)	4,644,000
Decrease (increase) in income tax receivable	(359,000)	517,000	50,000
Decrease (increase) in other current assets	(390,000)	210,000	(162,000)
Decrease (increase) in other assets	(2,323,000)	181,000	634,000
Increase (decrease) in accounts payable	(274,000)	1,017,000	(2,800,000)
Increase (decrease) in accrued liabilities	(682,000)	1,302,000	(28,000)
Increase (decrease) in other long-term liabilities	(89,000)	376,000	(93,000)
Net cash provided by operating activities	2,156,000	881,000	5,646,000
Cash flows from investing activities:			
Net purchases of property, plant and equipment	(6,669,000)	(4,184,000)	(1,459,000)
Proceeds from sale of property, plant and equipment	8,000	46,000	1,000
Net cash used in investing activities	(6,661,000)	(4,138,000)	(1,458,000)
Cash flows from financing activities:			
Principal payments on capital lease obligations	(22,000)	(36,000)	(53,000)
Borrowings on line of credit	47,475,000	39,498,000	16,065,000
Payments on line of credit	(43,015,000)	(38,008,000)	(16,065,000)
Proceeds from long-term debt	3,000,000	1,441,000	—
Principal payments on notes payable and long-term debt	(3,301,000)	(865,000)	(887,000)
Proceeds from exercise of stock options	740,000	—	—
Treasury stock acquired	(479,000)	(3,133,000)	(1,429,000)
Net cash provided by (used in) financing activities	4,398,000	(1,103,000)	(2,369,000)
Effect of exchange rate changes on cash	(69,000)	(916,000)	(75,000)
Net (decrease) increase in cash and cash equivalents	(176,000)	(5,276,000)	1,744,000
Cash and cash equivalents, beginning of year	1,231,000	6,507,000	4,763,000
Cash and cash equivalents, end of year	$ 1,055,000	$ 1,231,000	$ 6,507,000
Supplemental disclosure of cash flow information:			
Interest paid	$ 1,352,000	$ 640,000	$ 431,000
Income taxes paid, net of refunds	2,248,000	3,903,000	2,400,000
Supplemental disclosures of noncash transactions:			
Capital lease equipment acquired and related capital lease obligations	163,000	—	—

See accompanying notes to consolidated financial statements.

5.) A Word on Computers, Computer Software, and Hand-Written Ledgers

("Obstacles are those frightful things you see when you take your eyes off the goal." - Henry Ford)

I think most of us are familiar with computers and all the things they can do. We are also too familiar with all the frustrations that come along with what are, on the one hand, amazing machines, yet on the other, often clunky and awkward to use.

If you don't have a computer, can't afford one, or simply don't want to use a computer for doing your books — that's fine. If you are a solo teacher and just starting out, a wired-spiral notebook and a pencil (and maybe a calculator) are all that you need for the 'books' of your business. Use your notebook to at least keep track of income and expense items using a format similar to the ledgers we looked at. Cash flow projections are also worth trying; if nothing else they will give you a little peace of mind (as in -- Yes, I will be able to make it through next month).

Whether you use hand ledgers or computer software to keep track of your business, it is important to save all income and expense receipts. If you can, copy checks before you cash them. Stick all expense receipts in a big envelope or file folder, or shoe box, but save them. They will help you save money on taxes.

By and large, the more organized you are at the start, and the more organized you are on a regular basis, the easier it will be to understand where your business is at financially, and where it is headed. Also, organizing your records and paperwork from the start makes it easier (and less frantic) at tax time. One helpful idea is to organize your expense items in categories that mimic the 1040 Schedule C form (see below, we'll talk a bit about taxes in the next section). This way, you have organized your expenses in the same categories that the IRS uses. You'll thank yourself at tax time, and your accountant will charge you less.

If you don't have a computer and are thinking about getting one, now is a great time to buy them. The PC industry is in the middle of a price war, and deals are everywhere. You can get a very good desktop for around $500 and a laptop for around $900. Dell Computer will even provide financing. Computers get easier to use and to learn with each passing year, and good tutorials usually come with your software.

If you already have a computer, consider getting some type of financial software for your personal and business use. *Quicken* (made by Intuit) makes simple and straightforward products that can keep track of multiple bank accounts, helps you reconcile the accounts, and even prints checks for you. Most importantly, once an item is entered in the program (assuming it is entered and identified correctly), it can be categorized and reported in any number of ways. **This is the outstanding benefit of programs such as *Quicken's*, and computing in general**.

There is little point in entering checks and amounts from your bank statement into a computer program if you will never look at them again. But for most of us, in our personal and business finances, we need to look at things in different ways, and itemize expenses by categories for taxes or planning purposes. This is where the programs can be of real benefit. For example, if you categorize a check as a business phone expense, *Quicken* will find it (whichever account it is in) and print it out in a report, on business expenses for example. You only need to use a program like this once to see its utility. These days most financial institutions, including credit card companies and banks, allow you to download your account transactions directly into Quicken, saving you the considerable time involved in hand-entering each transaction.

Below are a couple of examples of a Quicken register (checkbook) and a report. For more information on Quicken products, go to www.intuit.com. If your business is a bit more complicated than that of a solo yoga teacher, consider Quick Books. Again, this is available at www.intuit.com . Quick Books will handle almost all small-business accounting chores including: tracking inventory, paying bills, payroll functions, invoicing, and much more.

Finally, if you own a yoga studio or business, there are two great sources of management software made specifically for your needs. www.mindbodysoftware.com or www.theWellworks.com.

Whether you use paper and pencil or a computer program, your business life will be much, much easier if you keep accurate and up-to-date books right from the start of your new business.

Checklist question:

Should I consider getting financial software to help manage the 'books' of my business?

The Business of Yoga

Ashley Walker Bus Account

Ashley Walker Bus. Acct
10/11/2002

Date	Num	Transaction	Payment	C	Deposit	Balance
/4/2002	DEP	Account cat: Mrs Griffin, Private		R	60.00	2,878.03
9/4/2002	ATM	Wells Fargo Bank cat: Cash	100.00	R		2,778.03
9/10/2002	DEP	Account cat: Girls Inc., Class		R	80.00	2,858.03
9/10/2002	405	AT*T Wireless cat: Cell Phone	60.25	R		2,797.78
9/11/2002	406	Giam/Yoga Mats cat: Yoga Equipment	73.24	R		2,724.54
9/12/2002	DEP	Account cat: Mrs Griffin, Private		R	60.00	2,784.54
9/12/2002	DEP	Account cat: Brenda Rogers, Private		R	60.00	2,844.54
9/12/2002	407	Kinko's cat: Marketing/Flyers	14.50	R		2,830.04
9/19/2002	DEP	Account cat: Girls Inc., Class		R	80.00	2,910.04
9/19/2002	DEP	Account cat: Mrs Griffin, Private		R	60.00	2,970.04
9/19/2002	DEP	Account cat: Brenda Rogers, Private		R	60.00	3,030.04
9/19/2002	408	Title 9 Sports cat: Yoga:Clothing	45.54	R		2,984.50
9/23/2002	DEP	Account cat: Girls Inc		R	80.00	3,064.50
/25/2002	DEP	Account cat: Mrs Griffin, Private		R	60.00	3,124.50
9/30/2002	DEP	Account cat: Girls Inc., Class		R	80.00	3,204.50
9/30/2002	DEP	AT*T Wireless cat: Misc. Income		R	12.42	3,216.92

The Business of Yoga

```
Ashley Walker Bus. Acct                                                    10/11/02
                              Itemized Categories Report
                                9/1/02 Through 9/30/02
                                                                            Page 1

  Cat/Sub    Date    Num       Description           Memo          Clr    Amount

  INCOME

  Brenda Rogers, Private
            9/12/02  DEP    Account                                 R       60.00
            9/19/02  DEP    Account                                 R       60.00
  TOTAL Brenda Rogers, Private                                              120.00

  Girls Inc
            9/23/02  DEP    Account                                 R       80.00
  TOTAL Girls Inc                                                            80.00

  Girls Inc., Class
            9/10/02  DEP    Account                                 R       80.00
            9/19/02  DEP    Account                                 R       80.00
            9/30/02  DEP    Account                                 R       80.00
  TOTAL Girls Inc., Class                                                   240.00

  Misc. Income
            9/30/02  DEP    AT*T Wireless                           R       12.42
  TOTAL Misc. Income                                                         12.42

  Mrs Griffin, Private
            9/4/02   DEP    Account                                 R       60.00
            9/12/02  DEP    Account                                 R       60.00
            9/19/02  DEP    Account                                 R       60.00
            9/25/02  DEP    Account                                 R       60.00
  TOTAL Mrs Griffin, Private                                                240.00

  TOTAL INCOME                                                              692.42

  EXPENSES

  Cash
            9/4/02   ATM    Wells Fargo Bank                        R     -100.00
  TOTAL Cash                                                              -100.00

  Cell Phone
            9/10/02  405    AT*T Wireless                           R      -60.25
  TOTAL Cell Phone                                                          -60.25

  Marketing
            9/12/02  407    Kinko's                                 R      -14.50
  TOTAL Marketing                                                           -14.50

  Yoga:
    Clothing
            9/19/02  408    Title 9 Sports                          R      -45.54
    TOTAL Clothing                                                          -45.54
  TOTAL Yoga                                                                -45.54

  Yoga Equipment
            9/11/02  406    Giam/Yoga Mats                          R      -73.24
  TOTAL Yoga Equipment                                                      -73.24

  TOTAL EXPENSES                                                           -293.53

  TOTAL INCOME - EXPENSES                                                   398.89
```

The Business of Yoga

Ashley Walker Bus. Acct

```
                    Cash Flow Report
                   9/1/02 Through 9/30/02
```

10/11/02

Page 1

Category Description	9/1/02-9/30/02
INFLOWS	
Brenda Rogers, Private	120.00
Girls Inc	80.00
Girls Inc., Class	240.00
Misc. Income	12.42
Mrs Griffin, Private	240.00
TOTAL INFLOWS	692.42
OUTFLOWS	
Cash	100.00
Cell Phone	60.25
Marketing	14.50
Yoga:	
Clothing	45.54
TOTAL Yoga	45.54
Yoga Equipment	73.24
TOTAL OUTFLOWS	293.53
OVERALL TOTAL	398.89

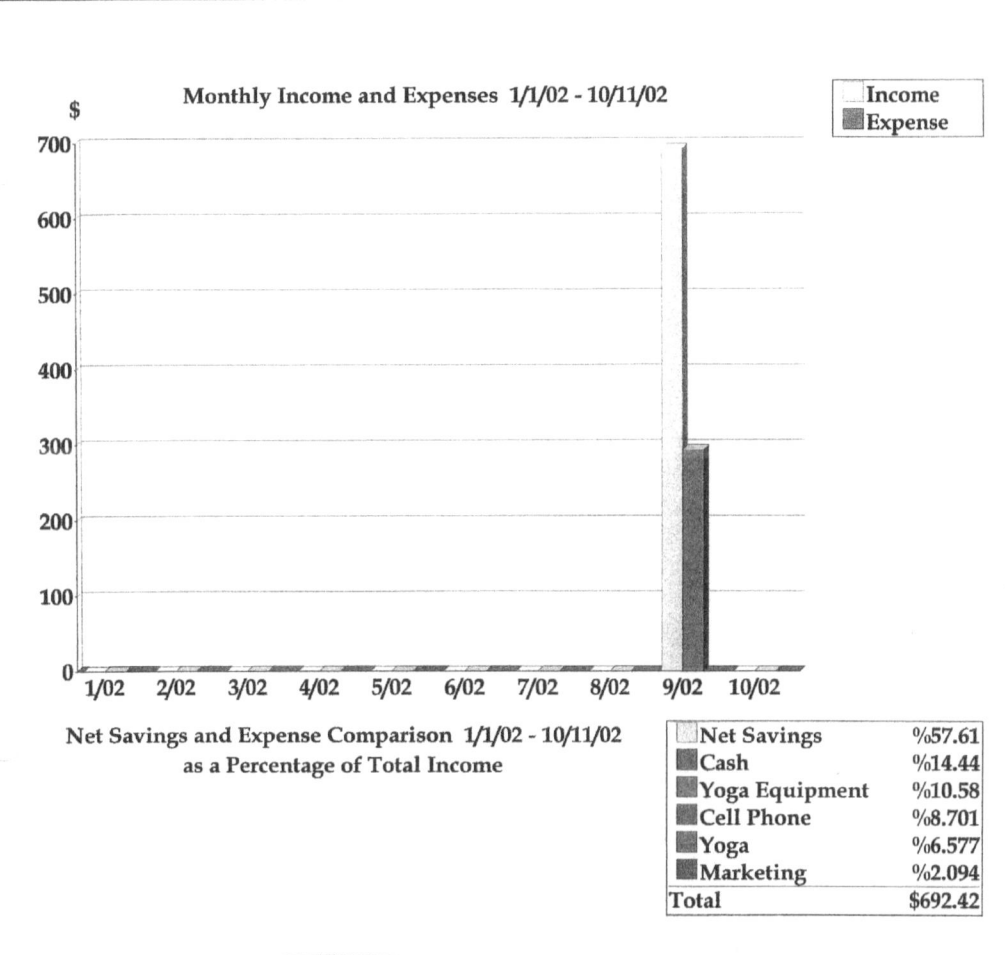

The Business of Yoga

Monthly Income and Expenses 1/1/02 - 10/11/02

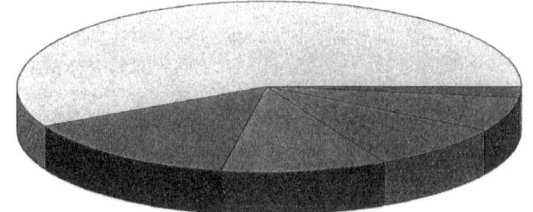

Net Savings and Expense Comparison 1/1/02 - 10/11/02 as a Percentage of Total Income

Net Savings	%57.61
Cash	%14.44
Yoga Equipment	%10.58
Cell Phone	%8.701
Yoga	%6.577
Marketing	%2.094
Total	$692.42

6.) A Primer on Sole Proprietorships and Tax Preparation

("Nothing is certain but death and taxes." – Benjamin Franklin)

This section is meant to give you a brief and general discussion about sole proprietorships and tax preparation. The section is mostly designed to show you where to go for help and what to look out for as you start your new business. <u>To understand the tax code and its impact on your business, you will need an accountant. Remember, ignorance of the tax code is not an excuse for failing to pay the taxes due. This section is meant as an introduction only and is not a substitute for tax planning and preparation.</u>

The simplest form of business entity is the sole proprietorship. For most of you starting out, whether as a solo teacher or a small business, this is where to begin. **If you choose this business structure, then legally speaking you and the business are the same.**

The chief advantage of a sole proprietorship is its simplicity. Unlike a corporation or an LLC, you do not have to file articles of incorporation and incur initial and ongoing attorney's fees. Remember, though, you still may have to obtain a business license and file a fictitious name statement.

The disadvantage of a sole proprietorship is that its structure (again, since you and the business are one) offers no inherent liability protection. As a solo yoga teacher this is often OK, as your services are generally protected by your professional liability insurance. (I noticed that in the Garden Way Yoga business plan (Part I), the business was set up as a sole proprietorship. In that case, given the complexity of the organization, that business needs to have a corporate or LLC structure to give the owner additional liability protection.)

For income taxes, a sole proprietor and its owner are treated as a single entity. Business profits and losses are reported on your own federal tax return, on Form 1040 Schedule C. If your business shows a loss, often times you are able to use it to offset other income on your 1040 return.

As you probably know, the tax code is incredibly complex and the maze of rules and regulations is ridiculously long. To make it worse, the tax code is constantly changing, so what is true one year may not be so the next year. And state tax code often differs from the federal tax codes. You most likely have experience filing personal taxes and have some idea of what's involved and where to get help. <u>Although the tax code is unmercifully frustrating and confusing, it is still your responsibility (and often to your financial advantage) to keep up on the current tax law as an individual and a small-business owner.</u>

Fortunately, there are lots of resources to help as you start your small business. The IRS puts out lots of free tax information as well as a **Tax Guide for Small Business**, and numerous free small-business publications. These generally provide reliable information (after all it is straight from the source). You can access these pamphlets, tax forms, and other information at (you guessed it) **www.irs.gov**. **You can also phone their toll free number, but you may not want to rely on information given over the phone. (With written matter, there is no confusion or misunderstanding-- and you can point to it, "see it's here in black and white!").**

There is also excellent computer software available for your personal and small business tax preparation and filings. Quicken and Turbotax are two popular and well-regarded programs, and the programs will help you prepare both federal and state tax returns. Again, go to www.intuit.com for information on these programs. There are also inexpensive tax services such as H&R Block.

However, of all the choices available, working with a good accountant is your best bet. Many accountants will charge only a few hundred dollars to do your personal taxes, if your financial situation is fairly simple. If you are adding on a part-time business as a yoga instructor, or starting out as a solo yoga teacher, your accountant may not charge a lot more to prepare a Schedule C (Sole Proprietorship) Form for you.

If you are not good at wading through tax codes and are planning to grow your business in the years to come, finding and working with a good accountant is well worth the money, and one of the best business decisions you will make. Still, even if you work with an accountant it is a good idea to get familiar with some of the tax issues. **As you start your small business it is a great idea to pay quarterly estimates of all the taxes you will owe for any particular year**. **(Go to www.irs.gov and click on Forms and then select 1040-ES for these forms and instructions.)** These estimates are due at the end of each quarter of your tax year, which for most individuals and small businesses is the calendar year (that is, ending on December 31st). This is a sort of "pay as you go" program that keeps you current on your taxes and helps prevent a "cash crunch" and tax penalties when the full amount of taxes fall due. Keeping up-to-date books on your business will help you and your accountant make appropriate estimate payments.

On your Schedule C Form it is important to record all the income and expenses incurred in your business for the particular tax year. As you can see on the form, all qualifying expenses are deducted from the business's gross income, **before** your personal income tax is computed. There are hundreds of expenses that can be deducted on your return, but while some are 100% deductible, some are not, and other expenses are depreciated over time. Be sure to keep receipts on any items that might be tax deductible. A business credit card (and the monthly itemized statements) makes this easy. It is in these sorts of areas that an accountant is well worth his fee. **While tax evasion is illegal, any business owner should make certain that he takes every deduction that he is legally allowed.**

As you look over the 1040 Schedule C form that follows, think about all of the expenses your business will incur. There's a good chance that a part or all of each expense is tax deductible.

Here's a list of business expense areas that may be fully or partially deductible (again each year you will need to get up to date and accurate information from the IRS):

- Advertising/Marketing
- Bad debts
- Car/Truck expenses (gas & service)
- Commission & fees
- Depreciation (of equipment)
- Employee benefit programs
- Insurance
- Mortgage
- Legal & professional services
- Office expense
- Rent or lease (vehicles or building)
- Repairs and maintenance
- Supplies
- Taxes and license
- Travel-Meals & entertainment
- Travel-Air, lodging, etc.
- Utilities (phone, etc.)
- Wages
- Other
- Expenses for business use of home

Checklist question:
Do I have adequate knowledge and/or help to prepare and pay my taxes?

The Business of Yoga

The Business of Yoga

The Business of Yoga

SCHEDULE C (Form 1040)
Department of the Treasury
Internal Revenue Service (99)

Profit or Loss From Business
(Sole Proprietorship)
▶ Partnerships, joint ventures, etc., must file Form 1065 or Form 1065-B.
▶ Attach to Form 1040 or Form 1041. ▶ See Instructions for Schedule C (Form 1040).

OMB No. 1545-0074
2001
Attachment Sequence No. 09

Name of proprietor | Social security number (SSN)

A Principal business or profession, including product or service (see page C-1 of the instructions) | B Enter code from pages C-7 & 8 ▶

C Business name. If no separate business name, leave blank. | D Employer ID number (EIN), if any

E Business address (including suite or room no.) ▶
City, town or post office, state, and ZIP code

F Accounting method: (1) ☐ Cash (2) ☐ Accrual (3) ☐ Other (specify) ▶
G Did you "materially participate" in the operation of this business during 2001? If "No," see page C-2 for limit on losses . ☐ Yes ☐ No
H If you started or acquired this business during 2001, check here . . . . ▶ ☐

Part I Income

1. Gross receipts or sales. Caution. If this income was reported to you on Form W-2 and the "Statutory employee" box on that form was checked, see page C-2 and check here . . . . . . ▶ ☐ | 1
2. Returns and allowances . . . . | 2
3. Subtract line 2 from line 1 . . . . | 3
4. Cost of goods sold (from line 42 on page 2) . . . . | 4
5. Gross profit. Subtract line 4 from line 3 . . . . | 5
6. Other income, including Federal and state gasoline or fuel tax credit or refund (see page C-3) . . . | 6
7. Gross income. Add lines 5 and 6 . . . . ▶ | 7

Part II Expenses. Enter expenses for business use of your home **only** on line 30.

8. Advertising . . . . . | 8
9. Bad debts from sales or services (see page C-3) . . | 9
10. Car and truck expenses (see page C-3) . . . | 10
11. Commissions and fees . . | 11
12. Depletion . . . . . . | 12
13. Depreciation and section 179 expense deduction (not included in Part III) (see page C-3) . . | 13
14. Employee benefit programs (other than on line 19) . . | 14
15. Insurance (other than health) . | 15
16. Interest:
    a Mortgage (paid to banks, etc.) . | 16a
    b Other . . . . | 16b
17. Legal and professional services . . . . . . | 17
18. Office expense . . . . | 18

19. Pension and profit-sharing plans | 19
20. Rent or lease (see page C-4):
    a Vehicles, machinery, and equipment . | 20a
    b Other business property . . | 20b
21. Repairs and maintenance . . | 21
22. Supplies (not included in Part III) . | 22
23. Taxes and licenses . . . . | 23
24. Travel, meals, and entertainment:
    a Travel . . . . | 24a
    b Meals and entertainment
    c Enter nondeductible amount included on line 24b (see page C-5) .
    d Subtract line 24c from line 24b | 24d
25. Utilities . . . . | 25
26. Wages (less employment credits) . | 26
27. Other expenses (from line 48 on page 2) . . . . | 27

28. Total expenses before expenses for business use of home. Add lines 8 through 27 in columns . . ▶ | 28
29. Tentative profit (loss). Subtract line 28 from line 7 . . . . | 29
30. Expenses for business use of your home. Attach **Form 8829** . . . . | 30
31. Net profit or (loss). Subtract line 30 from line 29.
    • If a profit, enter on **Form 1040, line 12**, and also on **Schedule SE, line 2** (statutory employees, see page C-5). Estates and trusts, enter on Form 1041, line 3.
    • If a loss, you **must** go to line 32. | 31
32. If you have a loss, check the box that describes your investment in this activity (see page C-6).
    • If you checked 32a, enter the loss on **Form 1040, line 12**, and also on **Schedule SE, line 2** (statutory employees, see page C-5). Estates and trusts, enter on Form 1041, line 3.
    • If you checked 32b, you **must** attach **Form 6198**. | 32a ☐ All investment is at risk.
    32b ☐ Some investment is not at risk.

For Paperwork Reduction Act Notice, see Form 1040 instructions. Cat. No. 11334P Schedule C (Form 1040) 2001

©Astraea Corp. 2005 pg. 131

The Business of Yoga

Schedule C (Form 1040) 2001 — Page 2

Part III — Cost of Goods Sold (see page C-6)

33 Method(s) used to value closing inventory: a ☐ Cost b ☐ Lower of cost or market c ☐ Other (attach explanation)

34 Was there any change in determining quantities, costs, or valuations between opening and closing inventory? If "Yes," attach explanation . . . . ☐ Yes ☐ No

35 Inventory at beginning of year. If different from last year's closing inventory, attach explanation . .

36 Purchases less cost of items withdrawn for personal use . . . .

37 Cost of labor. Do not include any amounts paid to yourself . . . .

38 Materials and supplies . . . .

39 Other costs . . . .

40 Add lines 35 through 39 . . . .

41 Inventory at end of year . . . .

42 Cost of goods sold. Subtract line 41 from line 40. Enter the result here and on page 1, line 4 . .

Part IV — Information on Your Vehicle. Complete this part **only** if you are claiming car or truck expenses on line 10 and are not required to file Form 4562 for this business. See the instructions for line 13 on page C-3 to find out if you must file.

43 When did you place your vehicle in service for business purposes? (month, day, year) ▶ ..../......./.......

44 Of the total number of miles you drove your vehicle during 2001, enter the number of miles you used your vehicle for:

a Business .... b Commuting .... c Other ....

45 Do you (or your spouse) have another vehicle available for personal use? . . . . ☐ Yes ☐ No

46 Was your vehicle available for personal use during off-duty hours? . . . . ☐ Yes ☐ No

47a Do you have evidence to support your deduction? . . . . ☐ Yes ☐ No

b If "Yes," is the evidence written? . . . . ☐ Yes ☐ No

Part V — Other Expenses. List below business expenses not included on lines 8–26 or line 30.

48 Total other expenses. Enter here and on page 1, line 27 . . . .

Schedule C (Form 1040) 2001

The Business of Yoga

PART III WORKSHOP

On the pages that follow you will find simple (but blank) income, expense and profit and loss spreadsheets that project out for the years 2005, 2006, 2007. Choose either a solo yoga teaching business, a teacher with a rental space and overhead, or whatever business you are planning.

Try to resist just throwing in any old numbers, but instead think hard and honestly about the business you might want to create. Make some guesses about income and <u>all</u> the expenses your business will have. Use the expense list on page 21 and the 1040 Form Schedule C to help with expense ideas.

Categorize the expenses on the expense spreadsheet and plug in your best guesses for the cost of them. When you are done, transfer them over to the Profit & Loss Statement spreadsheet. Try to be realistic about income and thorough with expenses. <u>**The point here is not to quickly fill in numbers but, rather, to take your time and try to construct a well thought out numerical picture of your business, and where it is headed.**</u>

The Business of Yoga

INCOME LEDGER   <u>2005</u>   <u>2006</u>   <u>2007</u>

INCOME

Q-1   Classes
       Privates

       Other

Q-2   Classes
       Privates

       Other

Q-3   Classes
       Privates

       Other

Q-4   Classes
       Privates

       Other

       Total Taxable Gross Income

EXPENSE
LEDGER   2005   2006   2007

EXPENSES

Total Taxable Gross Income

The Business of Yoga

PROFIT & LOSS LEDGER   2005   2006   2007

INCOME
Classes
Private Instruction
Other
TOTAL INCOME

EXPENSES

TOTAL EXPENSES

Net Pre-tax Income
(Income-Expenses

PART IV

1.) Growing Your Business
   ("Knowledge speaks, but wisdom listens" –Jimi Hendrix)

To Grow Your Business, *Listen* -Throughout this course we have touched on many of the attitudes, methods, and tools that are needed to run a successful business. **No tools are more important in business than the abilities to: listen, learn, and adapt.**

Listening is a lost art. **Active listening is a gift that we should all work to acquire, and an edge that all small-business owners must have**. In our contemporary world there is so much thrown at us, so much noise, that our senses learn to tune a lot of it out. Multi-tasking has made the situation worse. Many of us are becoming experts at half-listening and still functioning. By habit, we get so used to tuning out the 'noise,' that we tune out the 'signal' as well. Listening is important, not only in your business, but in all areas of life.

As a yoga teacher you learn to listen to your students. As a small-business owner you need to listen to them not only as students, but as customers. What do they like? What do they not like? The smallest comment can be loaded with information. Is a student mentioning another teacher or another studio more and more often? Are students at your studio complaining about one teacher repeatedly canceling classes on short notice? Are you getting lots of compliments since you changed the sequencing in class? Is another teacher at your studio dropping hints about leaving? In these instances and others, listen for information that can help you improve your teaching, and improve your business. Also, learn to tune in to more subtle signs and your inner voice. Remember the porpoises from the sea story in Part 1. Are events or feelings sending you in one direction over another?   I'm not one for going off on whims, but I try to pay attention. There is a lot of useful information out there; 'signal' within the 'noise.' Develop ways to listen for it and learn from it.

Learn - Develop the habit of being an active student of life and business. Go to yoga conferences. Take classes from teachers who have different styles and disciplines than your own. Talk to other teachers and studio owners about their business experiences. Talk with other small-business owners. **Be critical and objective about what you know, what you don't know, and what you need to learn**.

Adapt - A business should be constantly learning and evolving. Like life, business is dynamic. An often mistaken notion of Darwin's theory, 'the survival of the fittest,' is the idea that this means the biggest, the strongest, or the most prolific. I think the 'fittest' in Darwin's view are those species that can best adapt. As we have seen, this is a useful trait for businesses. (Hawaii Jack, Pacific West Water, & Ashley Walker are all good examples of this.) **As Darwin said, "It is not the strongest species that survive nor the most intelligent, but the most responsive to change." In our world of economic Darwinism, that's a good thought to hold on to.** Listening, learning and adapting are all traits that will help you grow your business, because, once developed, they will help you pursue good opportunities, and avoid trouble.

Grow your business step-by-step - Just as you need to take some time to think about going into business, you also need to think carefully about growing and expanding your business. There are a number of things to watch out for.

First and foremost – is it something **you** want to do? If a new project or opportunity is going to take you in directions that you don't like and you may not be good at – well, think twice. **You may love teaching yoga and you may be terrific at it. This doesn't mean you should open a studio**. You may like teaching and enjoy the freedom that it provides. You have time off when you want, and it is a simple business to run. You may hate being the boss, hiring (and firing) teachers, overseeing a payroll, and worrying about paying the rent. In that case, why take it on. Any business expansion brings more paperwork, more responsibility, and more financial commitments. Caution is in order here, and you might think about the idea of small steps.

The 'Ashley-Walker' model is good, in one way, because it is so comfortable. Each step is a small one and is comfortable for our fictional teacher on a personal and financial level. At almost any step along the way, she can go back to where she started, back off a bit on teaching, or go up a step and teach more. **She controls her business destiny. Contrast this with quitting your job, taking your savings or borrowing money and opening a studio – having never run one before**. At best it has to be nerve wracking, at worst you will have a horrible experience and lose your money. The sections that follow deal with various aspects of growing your business such as leasing space and dealing with employees.

2.) Getting a Roof over Your Business
(Location, Location, Location – every real estate agent, I've ever met)

One important tenet of business is maintaining a low overhead. If you pay attention to costs and expenses (bookkeeping does have a purpose), more money goes to the bottom line when times are good. And when they're not so good, well-- low overhead helps in 'stormy weather.' Rent space, or open a studio, only when your business demands it, when the marketplace gives you permission. Don't do it to feed your ego, or because (at the moment) you have the money. Do it because you have built up enough of a client base to support the location. Do it because there is a real need for your vision and how you want to teach, and there is no place to teach it.

Location, Location, Location - Real estate agents always talk about location, location, location, and with good reason. Often times the location will help make the business a success, or sink it. Again, be your clients. What do they need? What do they want? What should you provide for them? Whether you are renting a space for classes or opening a full-time center here are a few things to keep in mind.

Your studio should be in a safe area of town. If you hold classes in the evening, make sure the exterior area has good lighting. The studio will need restrooms. If they are shared with others in the building, make sure they are safe and available at the times you will need them. Remember, you will have a lot of students using them and changing in them. If at all possible, your studio should have some kind of lobby, or a café nearby where students can wait indoors before classes and get grounded and ready for the outside world (especially driving) after classes. The studio should have plenty of parking, and be accessible by bike or public transportation. (Let's support alternative transportation!) If possible it should be near the center of town (or a central point that is close and convenient for a lot of people).

Go to the location you are considering at different times of the day, and different days of the week. What seems calm and tranquil at 10 am on a Saturday morning may not be so on a Monday morning. Take notice of what businesses are around you. Will they generate noises or odors (good or bad) that will be a distraction or an annoyance? (A bakery or a Starbucks will have great smells, but they might be distracting.)

There will always be trade-offs. The best choice may be more than you can afford, though sometimes it may be worth stretching your budget for a better location. The superior location may draw more students and attention, and you won't have to move up to it later. Just make sure you can pay for it. **The fun and the challenge of small-business decisions is that they are a continuous balancing act.**

Remember Stir Crazy Coffee? Don't think about opening a new studio next to a well-established one, unless you are willing to compete directly with them, or they have more students than they can handle. Wherever you go, make sure the area can support your yoga studio. Where I live we had two public golf courses in town: one, more expensive and on the seacoast; the other, a bit smaller and in the center of town. They co-existed for years and made money. Two new courses were built a few years ago, and a price war started up. More importantly, suddenly four courses were now vying for a golfing public that had supported two. Two of the courses are now in bankruptcy.

A useful and sometimes overlooked alternative to renting your own space is to sub-lease from someone else, on an hourly basis. This is a great and economical way to start out. You might find that a dance studio has unused time available, and the owner is willing to charge you an hourly rate for just the time you are teaching classes. Even the math here is simple. If you can rent the space for $50 dollars per class, and charge your students $10 — well you're making money when the sixth student walks through the door. If you are lucky enough to find such an arrangement, insist on a written agreement so that there are no misunderstandings.

When you lease (or rent) space, attention to detail and persistence are crucial. Every lease is a little different, and it is important to know what you are getting for your money, what you are responsible for, and what your landlord is responsible for.

A lease can seem as simple as renting your neighbor's empty garage to hold classes in. But even here the devil is in the details. Do zoning laws allow this? Who pays for heat? Can either party back out? If so, how and when? Does your lease include the use of the bathroom off the garage? Who keeps it clean and stocks it? What about liability insurance? What if one of your students backs her car over your neighbor's fence, cat, or child? The neighbor says his garage is 600 sq. ft., but the first day of class you find it is hard to fit five students in it. What happens now?

Understanding what you are in for when you lease a space is obviously important, and that means being able to understand and negotiate lease agreements.

A lease is simply a contract between you and the landlord. Leases and rental agreements are sometimes used interchangeably, but generally a lease is a written long-term agreement. The lessor is the landlord, the lessee is the tenant. In theory all terms of a lease are negotiable, but a lot depends on the prevailing economic conditions.

If you can, find out as much about any property you are considering before you start talking with the landlord. Does he need the cash? Is he having trouble renting the property? Have other properties on the block gone quickly? Is there a high turn-over rate? Next, think about what you should ask for. What is really important to you? A lower rent is always on everyone's wish list, but what about modifications to the space that the landlord pays for? A new floor? Better heat? Sometimes if a landlord is unwilling to reduce the rent, he might help out with the remodeling costs (often called build-outs) that are worth as much or more than the rent reduction you were seeking.

Here are a few things to watch out for when you are shopping for a lease.

Make sure the correct people or business entities sign the lease. In other words, make sure that the person or legal entity that is signing you to a lease is the owner of the property, or has the legal authority to do so, and if in doubt ask for documentation.

Be sure you sign the lease correctly. If you are signing as a business entity such as a corporation, be sure it is clear you are signing on behalf of the Corporation, for example, Bob Jones, President of ABC Corp. **If you sign as an individual or as a sole proprietorship, know that you are personally on the hook for the life of that lease.** If you are asked to personally guarantee the lease, make sure you know what you are on the hook for. Three months might be an acceptable risk to you, three years might not be.

Know exactly what you are leasing. The lease should identify the space you are occupying. If there are common areas that you share with other tenants (hallways, elevators, restrooms, etc.), make sure your use of them is clearly spelled out in the lease, especially if you are teaching classes in the evenings and on weekends.

Find out how the square footage for the lease is calculated (inside wall, outside wall?), and go measure the space on your own. Make sure your calculations and the ones the landlord has given you are the same. If they are different, it may be that you are paying for a share of the commons area, something you need to know. If your lease includes parking spaces or inside storage, make sure that they are spelled out in the lease as well.

Have a start date for your lease. This start date should be clearly stated in the lease, and there should be some kind of penalty, or incentive to make sure you can be up and running on that date. Without a clear deadline and penalty your landlord may be slow to get the old tenant out or finish any work that is being done. Negotiate a cut-off date, a date you can cancel the lease if the space is not ready for you. If the space you are renting is in a building under construction, make sure your lease cannot begin until local building officials have issued a certificate of occupancy for the building. With space that is currently vacant, see if the landlord will give you immediate access to paint and decorate, so you can be up and in business when the lease begins.

Think about an Option to Renew. If you like the space you are leasing, and think the location is important to your business, consider asking for an option to renew at the time you sign your lease. For example, you may not want to sign a four-year lease until you are certain your business will succeed, yet a two-year lease with an option for another two years might feel right. Ask the landlord. It is not usually in his best economic interest to give you the option, so you may have to pay a bit more for it. But it does give you flexibility and locks in your location.

Be sure to look at the space carefully and ask lots of questions before you sign the lease. When you visit the space, take a tape measure, and measure the square footage yourself. Figure that you will need around 30 sq ft. (a 5 ft. by 6 ft. space) per student. Are the walls unencumbered and usable? Does the roof leak? Are the air conditioning/heating, plumbing, and electrical all in working order? Are the utilities on a separate meter from other tenants? Who is responsible and pays for painting and remodeling? If you do so, are you obligated to restore the area to its original condition when you leave? What will that cost? Try and have several meetings with your landlord or a period of time. When you think of questions, write them down. Be honest and detailed in telling the landlord what you are planning. If you're putting in a back area that has washing machines, ask your landlord, "Who is responsible for flooding?" Don't accept vague answers. See if you can meet the other tenants. Get to know them and their businesses. Let them know what you are doing. Make sure all of you can co-exist.

Take a trip down to the County Clerk's office and make sure the zoning laws work with your plans. **The goal here is to expose any problems, before you sign the lease.** I've included a standard commercial lease form for your reference on starting on page 144.

Above all, if you do not completely understand the lease and what you are getting into, don't sign it. Having an attorney review any lease is always a good idea.

A Simple Way to Price Rental Space.   Here's a great example of the help you can get by kicking around the numbers. There is always some guesswork involved in business, and that will certainly be the case if you rent studio space. But some simple math will help you see if what you are doing is realistic.

Say that you've been teaching at a yoga studio for several years and for various reasons want to teach from your own space. You've found a great space in a shared building for $1500 month and you're responsible for utilities, which run about $150 per month. The space was a dance studio and is perfect for a yoga studio. You will need renter's property damage liability insurance for $600 per year (or $50 per month). The space is 30 x 30 ft. and all the wall space is usable. In your community you can charge about $10 per student. Since these expenses total $1700 per month, you will need to teach 170 students in that month, just to cover your rental. (1700/10). The room will probably hold up to 30 students. (900 sq.ft./30 sq. ft.) If you can get 10 students for each class, that works out to 17 classes per month, or a little over 4 a week. **That's what it takes to cover just the cost of the studio, though you're not making money yet.**

Put another way:

$1500 + $150 + $50 = $1,700 – The cost of the space

$10 (per student) * 170 = $1,700 – Income necessary to cover the cost of the space

$10 (student) * 10 (students per class) * 17 (classes per month) = $1,700

Once you plug in the numbers like this, you get a picture and some information. While nothing is exact, you at least know if you're in the ballpark. (Yes, I think I can get that many students. Yes, I can teach four classes a week.) Don't forget about holidays (when attendance is down,) or the month you spend in the south of France. Remember these figures do not take into account, other expenses: your cell phone, car maintenance, flyers and advertising, etc., let alone give you any income. As simple as this is, it's good to put it down on paper, and see the numbers in black and white. It helps remove the emotion whether it is good (I love the place, I've got to have it) or bad (I'm scared of renting my own space). Playing with the numbers really helps you see what is possible and realistic, and what is not.

LF140-04
R140-04

COMMERCIAL LEASE

This lease is made between   ,
of   ,
herein called Lessor, and   ,
of   ,
herein called Lessee.
Lessee hereby offers to lease from Lessor the premises situated in the City of   , County of   , State of   ,
described as

upon the following TERMS and CONDITIONS:

1. Term and Rent. Lessor demises the above premises for a term of   years, commencing   , 20   , and terminating on   , 20   , or sooner as provided herein at the annual rental of   Dollars ($), payable in equal installments in advance on the first day of each month for that month's rental, during the term of this lease. All rental payments shall be made to Lessor, at the address specified above.

2. Use. Lessee shall use and occupy the premises for   . The premises shall be used for no other purpose. Lessor represents that the premises may lawfully be used for such purpose.

3. Care and Maintenance of Premises. Lessee acknowledges that the premises are in good order and repair, unless otherwise indicated herein. Lessee shall, at his own expense and at all times, maintain the premises in good and safe condition, including plate glass, electrical wiring, plumbing and heating installations and any other system or equipment upon the premises and shall surrender the same, at termination hereof, in as good condition as received, normal wear and tear excepted. Lessee shall be responsible for all repairs required, excepting the roof, exterior walls, structural foundations, and:

which shall be maintained by Lessor. Lessee shall also maintain in good condition such portions adjacent to the premises, such as sidewalks, driveways, lawns and shrubbery, which would otherwise be required to be maintained by Lessor.

4. Alterations. Lessee shall not, without first obtaining the written consent of Lessor, make any alterations, additions, or improvements, in, to or about the premises.

5. Ordinances and Statutes. Lessee shall comply with all statutes, ordinances and requirements of all municipal, state and federal authorities now in force, or which may hereafter be in force, pertaining to the premises, occasioned by or affecting the use thereof by Lessee.

6. Assignment and Subletting. Lessee shall not assign this lease or sublet any portion of the premises without prior written consent of the Lessor, which shall not be unreasonably withheld. Any such assignment or subletting without consent shall be void and, at the option of the Lessor, may terminate this lease.

7. Utilities. All applications and connections for necessary utility services on the demised premises shall be made in the name of Lessee only, and Lessee shall be solely liable for utility charges as they become due, including those for sewer, water, gas, electricity, and telephone services.

8. Entry and Inspection. Lessee shall permit Lessor or Lessor's agents to enter upon the premises at reasonable times and upon reasonable notice, for the purpose of inspecting the same, and will permit Lessor at any time within

Rev. 10/01

© 1992-2001 Made E-Z Products, Inc.
This product does not constitute the rendering of legal advice or services. This product is intended for informational use only and is not a substitute for legal

sixty (60) days prior to the expiration of this lease, to place upon the premises any usual "To Let" or "For Lease" signs, and permit persons desiring to lease the same to inspect the premises thereafter.

9. Possession. If Lessor is unable to deliver possession of the premises at the commencement hereof, Lessor shall not be liable for any damage caused thereby, nor shall this lease be void or voidable, but Lessee shall not be liable for any rent until possession is delivered. Lessee may terminate this lease if possession is not delivered within _____ days of the commencement of the term hereof.

10. Indemnification of Lessor. Lessor shall not be liable for any damage or injury to Lessee, or any other person, or to any property, occurring on the demised premises or any part thereof, and Lessee agrees to hold Lessor harmless from any claims for damages, no matter how caused.

11. Insurance. Lessee, at his expense, shall maintain plate glass and public liability insurance including bodily injury and property damage insuring Lessee and Lessor with minimum coverage as follows:

> Lessee shall provide Lessor with a Certificate of Insurance showing Lessor as additional insured. The Certificate shall provide for a ten-day written notice to Lessor in the event of cancellation or material change of coverage. To the maximum extent permitted by insurance policies which may be owned by Lessor or Lessee, Lessee and Lessor, for the benefit of each other, waive any and all rights of subrogation which might otherwise exist.

12. Eminent Domain. If the premises or any part thereof or any estate therein, or any other part of the building materially affecting Lessee's use of the premises, shall be taken by eminent domain, this lease shall terminate on the date when title vests pursuant to such taking. The rent, and any additional rent, shall be apportioned as of the termination date, and any rent paid for any period beyond that date shall be repaid to Lessee. Lessee shall not be entitled to any part of the award for such taking or any payment in lieu thereof, but Lessee may file a claim for any taking of fixtures and improvements owned by Lessee, and for moving expenses.

13. Destruction of Premises. In the event of a partial destruction of the premises during the term hereof, from any cause, Lessor shall forthwith repair the same, provided that such repairs can be made within sixty (60) days under existing governmental laws and regulations, but such partial destruction shall not terminate this lease, except that Lessee shall be entitled to a proportionate reduction of rent while such repairs are being made, based upon the extent to which the making of such repairs shall interfere with the business of Lessee on the premises. If such repairs cannot be made within said sixty (60) days, Lessor, at his option, may make the same within a reasonable time, this lease continuing in effect with the rent proportionately abated as aforesaid, and in the event that Lessor shall not elect to make such repairs which cannot be made within sixty (60) days, this lease may be terminated at the option of either party. In the event that the building in which the demised premises may be situated is destroyed to an extent of not less than one-third of the replacement costs thereof, Lessor may elect to terminate this lease whether the demised premises be injured or not. A total destruction of the building in which the premises may be situated shall terminate this lease

14. Lessor's Remedies on Default. If Lessee defaults in the payment of rent, or any additional rent, or defaults in the performance of any of the other covenants or conditions hereof, Lessor may give Lessee notice of such default and if Lessee does not cure any such default within _____ days, after the giving of such notice (or if such other default is of such nature that it cannot be completely cured within such period, if Lessee does not commence such curing within such _____ days and thereafter proceed with reasonable diligence and in good faith to cure such default), then Lessor may terminate this lease on not less than _____ days' notice to Lessee. On the date specified in such notice the term of this lease shall terminate, and Lessee shall then quit and surrender the premises to Lessor, without extinguishing Lessee's liability. If this lease shall have been so terminated by Lessor, Lessor may at any time thereafter resume possession of the premises by any lawful means and remove Lessee or other occupants and their effects. No failure to enforce any term shall be deemed a waiver.

15. Security Deposit. Lessee shall deposit with Lessor on the signing of this lease the sum of _____ Dollars ($ _____) as security for the performance of Lessee's obligations under this lease, including without limitation the surrender of possession of the premises to Lessor as herein provided. If Lessor applies any part of the deposit to cure any default of Lessee, Lessee shall on demand deposit with Lessor the amount so applied so that Lessor shall have the full deposit on hand at all times during the term of this lease.

16. Tax Increase. In the event there is any increase during any year of the term of this lease in the City, County or State real estate taxes over and above the amount of such taxes assessed for the tax year during which the term of this lease commences, whether because of increased rate or valuation, Lessee shall pay to Lessor upon presentation of paid tax bills an amount equal to   % of the increase in taxes upon the land and building in which the leased premises are situated. In the event that such taxes are assessed for a tax year extending beyond the term of the lease, the obligation of Lessee shall be proportionate to the portion of the lease term included in such year.

17. Common Area Expenses. In the event the demised premises are situated in a shopping center or in a commercial building in which there are common areas, Lessee agrees to pay his pro-rata share of maintenance, taxes, and insurance for the common area.

18. Attorney's Fees. In case suit should be brought for recovery of the premises, or for any sum due hereunder, or because of any act which may arise out of the possession of the premises, by either party, the prevailing party shall be entitled to all costs incurred in connection with such action, including a reasonable attorney's fee.

19. Waiver. No failure of Lessor to enforce any term hereof shall be deemed to be a waiver.

20. Notices. Any notice which either party may or is required to give, shall be given by mailing the same, postage prepaid, to Lessee at the premises, or Lessor at the address specified above, or at such other places as may be designated by the parties from time to time.

21. Heirs, Assigns, Successors. This lease is binding upon and inures to the benefit of the heirs, assigns and successors in interest to the parties.

22. Option to Renew. Provided that Lessee is not in default in the performance of this lease, Lessee shall have the option to renew the lease for an additional term of   months commencing at the expiration of the initial lease term. All of the terms and conditions of the lease shall apply during the renewal term except that the monthly rent shall be the sum of $. The option shall be exercised by written notice given to Lessor not less than   days prior to the expiration of the initial lease term. If notice is not given in the manner provided herein within the time specified, this option shall expire.

23. Subordination. This lease is and shall be subordinated to all existing and future liens and encumbrances against the property.

24. Radon Gas Disclosure. As required by law, (Landlord) (Seller) makes the following disclosure: "Radon Gas" is a naturally occurring radioactive gas that, when it has accumulated in a building in sufficient quantities, may present health risks to persons who are exposed to it over time. Levels of radon that exceed federal and state guidelines have been found in buildings in   . Additional information regarding radon and radon testing may be obtained from your county public health unit.

25. Entire Agreement. The foregoing constitutes the entire agreement between the parties and may be modified only by a writing signed by both parties. The following Exhibits, if any, have been made a part of this lease before the parties' execution hereof:

Signed this   day of   , 20   .

By:_____ Lessor   By:_____ Lessee

Get the Necessary Insurance You can spend all your money on insurance. There are all types of business insurance available (because there are so many exclusions on policies). You'll need to find out what insurance the law requires, what is extremely important, what is needed by your landlord or lender, what you feel comfortable with, and what you can do without. You should not duplicate your landlord's insurance but you will need to augment it where necessary. You should be most concerned about liability insurance--that is, events you may be held responsible for, fire, flooding, etc. You might want business interruption insurance (if your building burns or is uninhabitable for a time, you may still have to pay rent). Remember, if a fire or flood starts in your space, you may be responsible for damage to others in the building. Do some comparison-shopping and just get the insurance you absolutely need.

Checklist question:

Have I thought through why I want to open my own yoga space, and if so, considered all of the potential problems and costs?

3.) Debts, Loans, & Leasing

("The problem with borrowed money is that it has to be repaid." – Someone I Know)

If there is any way to start your business and keep it growing without borrowing money — do it. The biggest problem with borrowed money is that eventually it (plus more money in the form of interest) has to be paid back. This is a loan's defining feature, and the one most people seem to forget.

For most small yoga businesses, borrowing money should not be necessary. If you need to get a big loan to rent studio space, maybe the space is too big to begin with. If you cannot cover your expenses as a solo yoga teacher, maybe your expenses are too high. In keeping with the step-by-step process above, it is more comfortable and probably a better business plan to rent space by the hour and build up your business and your bank account rather than borrowing money to lease a space.

The same method applies for your own studio. Why not open your studio with the profits you have saved from teaching, profits that prove you have a following? Start small and grow slowly.

If you absolutely need to borrow money, shop around and pay back the loan as quickly as possible. This will help you sleep better at night, and establish a good credit history for you and your business.

You will find that there are a number of public sources for loans, such as banks and government agencies that help small businesses (such as the Small Business Administration, go to www.sba.gov). Millions of dollars in government-backed loans --called 504s --go unused each year. Such loans will require a lot of paperwork, as well as a polished business plan. (The Garden Yoga business plan was written with this in mind.) There are usually private sources as well, such as family and friends.

Typically, there will be terms and conditions for the loan: benchmarks for the business's progress, how and when you will have to pay the loan back, and at what interest. Often, you will be required to personally put up collateral (something of value) that the loaner gets if you default on the loan. **Make sure you understand each and every aspect of a loan *before* you sign the papers.**

The same rules apply for leasing or buying equipment over time. If Dell will let you buy a computer over time for little interest and no pre-payment penalty — well, that might make sense.

The same is true in leasing a car, or buying one on payments. Know what you are getting into, and why you are doing it. If you need a car and don't have the money, leasing or buying a car with a loan may be your only option.

Remember that cars are depreciating assets (they lose value over time), so try to get just what is needed and let the other guy pay more money to make a fashion statement.

Here are some general rules for leasing vs. buying. Generally, your payments will be a third more if you buy (over time) than if you lease. With a lease you are not responsible for maintenance, so you save on those out-of-pocket expenses. Of course, when a buyer is finished with his payments, he will own the car free and clear. The leaser will own nothing, and will have to buy out the rest of his lease if he wants to keep the car. Generally, if you are planning to keep a car longer than three or four years, it makes sense to buy the car.

Whether you are leasing or buying, these days it is easy to do comparison-shopping on the Internet. There are a large number of sites for buying cars; two sites to try are **www.edmunds.com** and **www.CarWizard.com**.

For leasing try **www.LeaseWizard.com**. At this site you will get a number of different quotes on the car you are interested in, complete with the interest rate (called "money factors" in leasing), and the predicted value of the car at the end of the lease (the "residuals"). With this information in hand, you can go and see what various dealers are offering and compare prices.

4.) Other Business Structures

("Never mistake motion for action" –Ernest Hemingway)

Though we often think of AT&T or Ford when the word corporation comes up, a corporation is defined by structure not size. A small one-man business can be a corporation. Corporations do all the same things other businesses do; it's just that when a business becomes a corporation the rules and the game are a little different. **Most small businesses incorporate to take advantage of certain liability protections and specific tax savings.**

A corporation is recognized by law as a legal 'entity' (the term comes from the word 'corpus' or body), and is legally separated from its owners. A corporation files its own tax returns (unlike a Schedule C business that piggybacks on the tax return of its owner).

In recent years, state and federal law have made it much easier for corporations to be formed around a small number of people, or even a single incorporator. Corporate boards may have a single director and shareholder, and shareholders and directors can take action by unanimous written consent rather than holding formal meetings.

As a legally separate entity, the corporation affords some protection from liability and creditors, although the protections and exceptions are complex, and continually tested in the courts. Incorporating will not protect the small-business owner from certain personal responsibilities such as not having car insurance or breaking the law.

Deciding to incorporate when you are a small, closely held business should be made on a case-by-case basis. Often, the corporate shell may be unnecessary or not offer the protection or benefits you need.

For instance, for a small corporation, the majority owners may still have to personally guarantee any loan made to that corporation. Here the corporation offers no advantage over a sole proprietorship, as the owner is still personally responsible for the loan.

Often liability insurance can protect against business risks, so that a business can be structured as a sole proprietorship without worrying about unlimited personal liability. This is most often the case for a solo yoga teacher.

On the other hand, if you are the owner of several yoga studios, make and sell yoga clothing, have employees, and produce and market yoga videos, there are likely to be a number of reasons to incorporate.

This is certainly the case if you look closely at the Garden Way Yoga Business Plan (Part I). In the plan, the owner holds the business as a Schedule C Proprietorship, and in my view that is a mistake. While she probably has certain types of liability insurance, she has a lot of exposure with the retail business, the property and the yoga classes. I think incorporating might be worth the time and money.

While there are several door-front services that offer inexpensive legal work, including incorporating your business (*We the People* in my area), it is best to consult an attorney to determine if incorporating is right for your small business. In addition to advising you, he will help you determine if your corporate name is available for incorporation in your state, prepare the articles of incorporation, and pay the filing fees and franchise tax fees required. These fees vary from state to state but can be up to $1,000. Initial legal fees should run about the same.

In recent years a new business structure, the limited liability Corporation or LLC, has been introduced. The differences between this and a corporation can be subtle and will depend on your particular needs and circumstances, so again it is best to consult an attorney.

The other commonly used business structure is the Limited Partnership. This structure is often used when a number of partners put up money to fund a venture, but are not involved in day-to-day operations. In this structure they put their money at risk but have 'limited' liability or financial exposure to the venture. These deals and their agreements are complicated, and need the assistance of a qualified attorney.

If you go into a simple partnership with another partner who will put up half the money and work half the time, it still gets complicated, and your best bet is to get an attorney to draw up a solid agreement that protects everyone's interests.

<u>I strongly recommend consulting any attorney before forming any business partnership, or structure.</u>

5.) Employees, Leadership and Business Relationships

("Only the shallow know themselves. –Oscar Wilde")

When is it Time to Hire Employees? - There may be a point down the road in your business when it is time to consider taking on employees. Here are a couple of points to help you decide if taking on employees is right for you.

Keep a detailed record of your business activities for several weeks. See what parts of your job you like and want to do and what is revenue producing. What is the best use of your time? This is your job description. What is left might be work for an employee. For example, your log of business activities might reveal that you have a hard time keeping up with billing, or you are unable to answer phone calls during busy times of the day. These are business needs that might be best served by hiring someone.

Employees vs. Independent Contractors - For many small businesses, taking on employees is considered a last-ditch option, and with good reason. Taking on an employee means taking on a lot of new responsibilities. More and different paperwork is one of them. You will have to be responsible for getting the payroll out twice a month, withholding employees' tax, and dealing with the federal bureaucracy on employee issues including: unemployment insurance, workmen's compensation, benefits, training, employee safety, etc. You will have to do the hiring and firing. Most importantly, the business will now have a few more mouths to feed.

One way to grow your business and keep the headaches and risk to a minimum is by using consultants and 'independent contractors.' In essence, they technically work for themselves, but are hired by you to do a particular job. You pay them a flat fee, but they are not on your payroll, so you don't have to take care of wages, W-2 tax forms, medical care, or other assorted administrative duties. Most yoga studios that I have seen hire their teachers as independent contractors for this very reason. (Go to page 71 for our example of an independent contractor agreement.)

As a solo teacher, if you hire an accountant, an artist to do your flyer, or go to *Kinko's* for your business cards, you are, in large part, doing the same thing. It's a great way to keep down costs. (Imagine the money you would need, the employees required, and the hassle of keeping all these services under your one 'roof.') If you need someone to answer your phone during busy times or need help with bookkeeping and billing, consider hiring a part-time independent contractor.

Communicating in the Work Place - While most of you won't have to worry about employees for sometime, it is worthwhile early on to start thinking about business relationships, not only with eventual employees, but also with others in the business food chain. **While you want to lead by example, you also want to communicate by example.** Long before you ever have employees, you'll want to develop business communication skills that complement and augment your teaching skills. **The golden rule applies here as well. (Treat others, as you would like to be treated.) If you expect your landlord or the yoga studio you work at to be straightforward and compassionate with you--well then, don't you own them the same in return?**

Being good at communicating is every bit as important in business as it is in personal relationships. If you are mad at your landlord, or feel underpaid by your yoga studio, or think the teacher in the next room plays his music too loud, think about ways of solving the problem. Often (not always) the other person may not be aware of what they are doing. Communicating your wants and needs, speaking your truth, can help clarify the situation. <u>**In business, problem solving is *the* essential skill, and often problem solving comes down to good communication skills.**</u> While it doesn't always work (the other party can tell you to go to hell), if you communicate clearly you will develop a reputation for being honest and straight forward. People will know what you stand for, what issues are important to you, and that you communicate well. These traits can only help you in the business world.

These same skills are doubly important if you take on employees. Most employees appreciate a boss who clearly and consistently communicates what he wants. They respect a leader who thinks before acting, someone whose values are well-known and consistent, a leader who has integrity. People seem to expect this out of their employees; why should employees expect (or get) anything less from their boss?

One sure way to lose employees respect (and hurt your business) is to not understand their work because you don't understand their job. There is no quicker way to destroy morale than going around issuing orders on things you know little or nothing about. In small businesses, many owners, by necessity, start out doing everything until the business can support new hires. This is an organic process and extremely important, because the owner gains an understanding of every job and what is involved. Later on, when others are doing the jobs, 'the boss' can speak to them with some knowledge and authority, because he has walked in their shoes.

If you have never worked on the task in question, you'll have a tough time evaluating that end of the business. If you are lucky, you'll have a good employee who will do it right. If you're not and you have no interest or knowledge of the task, sooner or later it will blow up and end up back in your lap.

Many, many businesses get in trouble because the owner is completely wrapped up in his business, hates the numbers, and ignores the books, leaving them to others. This is always a mistake. It's your business and if you project a casual disinterest towards money and profits, so will your employees -- with disastrous results.

Checklist questions:

Is it time to hire employees, or can you work with independent contractors?
Are you leading by example and communicating clearly in all business relationships?

6.) Six Steps Towards Improving Your Business

("Perfection is achieved, not when there is nothing to add, but when there is nothing to take away." - Antoine de Saint Exupery)

Brand Your Business

In earlier sections, we talked about building a franchise or brand, so that you are competing on your name, service, and reputation -- not on price. **Building your business identity, your brand, is a career-long endeavor.**

Since no one person or business can be all things to all people, stay focused on what you stand for and what you want your business to be to its students and customers. Look at the mission statement and vision statement from your business plan. Is it what you and your business stand for?

Ask yourself: What does my business stand for? What do we hope to accomplish? How do I want my business to be perceived? Am I in the right niche for my business goals? How do I differentiate my business today? How will I in the future?

Every business, even teaching yoga, serves a certain part of the market, <u>not all of it</u>. Your goals for your business, your marketing, and your business niche should all be aligned towards building the brand or reputation you want.

If your goal is to make expensive, high-performance, cutting-edge surfboards for top-end surfers (as we saw in the earlier example), then that is what you work towards and build your brand on. You will make fewer but better surfboards and get some of the top professional surfers to ride your boards. You will not market your surfboards at Costco or produce large quantities of low-performance boards.

If, as a yoga teacher, you know that you want to build your reputation teaching seniors — go after that, and make sure all parts of your business are aligned towards building that brand and that reputation.

Clients or students help define the identity of your business. If you teach yoga more or less anonymously at the local YMCA, that will be your identity. If you teach yoga in Hollywood to stars and celebrities, that will be your reputation. If you teach seniors, that will be your reputation.

A consistent message is important in building a brand. Consistency equals comfort. Clients are assured that they can count on the same experience time after time. McDonalds is the obvious example of this. The taste and quality of the food is less important than knowing you can expect the same thing whether you go into a McDonalds in San Diego, New York or Omaha. (Yuck to many of us, McDonalds *is* consistent.)

Over time, your reputation might assure your yoga students that they can count on you to be on time, teach a terrific class, help individual students with specific adjustments, and help them grow and deepen their own practice. They will come back for these reasons, because they can count on your teaching—not because you charge three dollars more or less than the other instructor.

Build Excellent Client Relationships

Think about your favorite businesses. Why do you like them? Why do you keep going back to them? More than likely, they take exceptional care of you. Maybe, they will do whatever it takes to make sure that their clients are completely satisfied. Companies such as L.L. Bean and Nordstrom's guarantee complete satisfaction with their products. Their guarantee is simple: if you are not completely satisfied, for any reason, exchange the product for a full refund—period. This type of attitude goes a long way towards excellent customer relationships. It tells the customer they are important and the company will work hard to keep them happy. It also builds the company's brand and reputation.

An effective customer satisfaction policy lets the customer feel that they are encouraged to come forward with any problems, and that they have a real voice in their relationship with your company.

For your business, again, communication is essential. Encourage students to talk with you after class, about what they like and, more importantly, what they don't like. If you unexpectedly have to cancel a class, offer a free class to those students that would have come. Build your own 100% satisfaction guarantee and make sure your students know about it.

Use Your Time Efficiently

For many of us, especially the new small-business owner, time is at a premium. Wasted time can add up to lost profits in the business world. Just as important, wasted time can prevent you from taking the time off you need to relax, get centered and recharge. Here are some tips for better time management:

Develop a schedule that works for you and your needs, and stick to it. Working for yourself means lots of flexibility, but use that to your advantage, not to be on permanent vacation. If you like to practice and teach in the mornings, design your schedule that way. Try to bunch classes together so you are not making multiple daily trips to the yoga studio.

Always leave some time during the day or week open. That way, if a private lesson, a household emergency, or a surprise visit from a friend comes along, it won't upset your whole schedule.

Do your work when you are most productive. Again, you may like to teach in the morning, do paper work or lesson plans in the evening. If you are writing a book and two o'clock in the morning is when your creativity gets going, that's when you should write, provided you can still get up and teach your classes in top form.

Screen your calls. Return work calls during work, and calls to friends when it won't throw you off your schedule. Conversely, there may be an hour between classes that is a great time to return business calls.

Put a dollar value on your time. Figure out what an hour of your time is worth. This will make you thing twice about wasting time. Realize that taking time to walk on the beach is different than wasting time.

If you don't have a computer, get one. It will save you time on bookkeeping, letter writing, keeping address books current, research, organizing and filing-- the list goes on and on. Make sure you learn to backup your files, and keep your computer files organized.

Clean and organize as you go. This is obvious, but seldom done.

Prioritize. Don't try to do more in less time, focus on doing things of greater importance. You can't do everything *and* do everything well.

Farm out the things you can't do or don't want to do. Figure out the best use of your time and let someone else do the other things. This may be bookkeeping, or house cleaning -- anything that isn't worth your time.

Grow Your Revenues

Whether you are just starting out in business, or your existing business has been hit by new competition or an economic slump, here are a few ideas for gaining new clients.

Make sure you are reaching your target audience. If, like Ashley Walker, you are interested in teaching seniors, review your marketing strategy. Have you left out some retirement homes in your community? Are there health clubs or spas that cater to older people? Is there a community newsletter for seniors that your ads should be in? Are your advertising and marketing efforts aimed at your target audience and not being wasted elsewhere?

Diversify your customer base If you are a solo teacher and trying to build your practice, try working at different times and at different levels to build a more diverse student base. If you are a more experienced teacher, consider teaching workshops, or teaching at other locations, where there might be students that are not familiar with your work. Diversifying your student base will help you grow your business by exposing you to different types of students, and they to you. The new students you meet may in turn bring in friends as new students or as clients for private lessons. Referrals are an important part of any business, especially in yoga. A wide and diverse student base helps steady your business.

Offer Something extra Try to give your students an extra reason to take yoga from you. It may be that you offer intensive courses every other month, in addition to your regular classes. Or that you offer a class in tandem with another event, or that you work out a package with a local spa so that students can get a discount on massage or body work by taking your class. Some teachers offer yearly retreats at exotic locations, and give their students first choice or discounts to attend.

Keep learning Take seminars. Go to other yoga classes and other studios, and see what they are about. Read trade publications to keep up on new ideas. Go to other teacher's workshops. Make it a point to continue your yoga education. Your business and the yoga you teach can only benefit by looking outside your classroom or studio.

Bring More Dollars To The Bottom Line

Taking a hard look at your costs and expenses can bring more of your hard-earned top-line dollars to the bottom line and into your pocket. Poring over your books can be well worth your time. In fact, it can be just as important as bringing in new business. Look at the three simple examples below.

	A	B	C
Revenues	$100,000	$120,000	$100,000
Expenses	$70,000	$84,000	$50,000
Pre-Tax Income	$30,000	$36,000	$50,000
Tax (33%)	$10,000	$12,000	$16,666
Net Income	$20,000	$24,000	$33,334

In example A, revenues are $100,000. Expenses are 70% of revenues and net income is 20% of revenues. In Example B revenues have grown by 20%, expenses are still 70% and the tax rate is the same. Net income has increased by 4,000. In example C, revenues stay the same as in A, but expenses are cut by 20% to 50% of revenue. The increase in net income is dramatic and far greater than growing the top line in B. **Cutting expenses can have a big impact on your bottom line.**

As you start your business, get in the habit of looking closely at your expenses and keeping them as efficient as possible. Early on, there won't be many expenses and it will be easy to identify excesses. Developing this habit will pay off later as your business gets bigger and more complex. That is the time when keeping expenses in check will really help. As the example above shows, this can be more effective and may take less work than going out and drumming up new business.

The best time to look at expenses is when you are taking care of bills, deposits, and paperwork. While you've got your cell phone bill in front of you, phone to see if there is a better rate available. Are your utilities higher than last month, for no apparent reason? If you've got the payroll in front of you, take a moment to think about the contributions each employee makes to your business. Are there several people doing the same job? Is your business organized efficiently, so that information and tasks aren't passed back and forth unnecessarily, wasting time and money? Any time and everyday is the right time to think about expenses.

Make A New Business Plan

As we have discussed, business plans are written to chart how your business will get from Point A to Point B. Those points change over time. A plan that might work for a new business could need revising four years into the business. All the things you've learned in those four years might make your old plan irrelevant to where your business is today.

The goal of any business plan is to help you get from one point to the next, to establish goals and milestones and to flesh out problems and opportunities. Those all will necessarily change as the business grows and your view changes with that growth.

Dig out your old plan as a starting point and see what in it still applies to your business. See what needs changing. **It may be that your understanding of your industry and marketplace has broadened and deepened, and you can now see a niche for your business that your earlier inexperience overlooked.**

Business plans are not just for start-ups.

Checkpoint question:

What are some ways to improve my business?

7.) Putting It All Together

("Not everything that can be counted counts, and not everything that counts can be counted." - Albert Einstein)

We have looked into the many elements of running a small business. We have discussed whether or not running a small business is the right thing for you -- and, of course, that is something only you can decide. We have talked a bit about how to plan a business, start a business, run a business, and grow a business.

Listed below are all the checklist questions we developed as we worked through the various sections of this manual. They are put together here to help you plan and run your new business.

If you choose to go into business having a checklist, learning from others, picking up the tools of the trade and mastering them, are all important. **But at the top of the list are the intangible assets you bring to your business: attitude, integrity, and commitment, and a joy and love for what you do.**

Step-by Step Business Checklist

Part I

1.) Is going into business for myself something I want to do and can do?
2.) Why do I want to go into business? What am I going into business for?
3.) What can I learn about other businesses as I start and grow my own business?
4.) What money issues do I carry with me? What were my family's attitudes toward money & wealth? What are mine? If I could change one thing about my relationship with money, it would be
_____.
5.) Can I bring integrity, authenticity and purpose to my business?
6.) What are the ethics that I bring to my teaching and to my business?
7.) What attitudes am I bringing into my business?
8.) What information am I listening to? Is it noise or signal?
9.) Do I have a Business Plan? Is it well thought-out and written down? Do I have a reasonable grasp of what my business expenses and income will be going forward?

Part II

1.) Do I have business cards and an appropriate resume ready to go?
2.) How do I want to present myself to the yoga community and at job interviews?
3.) Does my studio (or do I) have appropriate sign-in and release sheets?
4.) Do I have adequate yoga liability insurance from a reliable company?
5.) Have I submitted all the necessary forms for my business to the appropriate agencies?
6.) Do I have a standardized contract for teaching at business and community locations?
7.) What will best suit my marketing needs? Do I need a Web site?

Step-by Step Business Checklist (cont.)

Part III

1.) Have I set up a checking account for my new business?
2.) Do I understand simple bookkeeping and its terminology?
3.) Can I set up simple ledgers and track income and expenses for my business?
4.) Should I consider getting financial software to help manage the 'books' of my business?
5.) Do I have adequate knowledge and help to prepare and pay my taxes?
6.) Have I thought about hiring an accountant for tax preparation and as an advisor?

Part IV

1.) Am I ready to listen, learn, and adapt as I grow my business?
2.) Have I thought through why I want to open a yoga space, and if so, considered most of the potential problems and cost?
3.) Am I comfortable with the legal structure of my business? Do I have adequate liability protections? Have I consulted an attorney?
4.) Is it time to hire employees, or can I work with independent contractors and consultants?
5.) Am I leading by example and communicating clearly in all business relationships?
6.) Am I working to build a brand in my business as well as terrific client relationships?
7.) Am I using my time efficiently?
8.) Am I growing my revenues by reaching my target audience, diversifying my customer base, and offering something extra?
9.) Can I cut my expenses and bring more dollars to the bottom line?
10.) Is it time to make a new business plan?

PART IV WORKSHOP

Take a few minutes to relax, and then write down five steps that you can take in the next month that will help you start or grow your business. Take your time and put some thought into the five steps you choose. <u>Make them simple and doable</u>.

APPENDICES

Nine Key Concepts to Remember

Start a business because you love what you are doing, and will enjoy working hard while you do it. Do what you love, love what you do. Business is about many things, making money is only one of them—and down the list at that.

Being a good human being is good business. Bring honesty, integrity, and authenticity to your business. (The Golden Rule applies.) Use small businesses to effect change.

Remember that You are the Business, and the Business is You. Everything and every person involved in your business reflects on you and your business—for better or worse.

Make everything as simple as possible—but not simpler. Get help when you need it. Set things up right from the start. Think and have a plan before you act.

Learn the tools, and the terms, and the rules of business. These are a must, if you want to play.

Remember the difference between involvement and commitment.

Listen, observe, adapt. "Watch for the porpoises." Be dynamic and creative.

Never, ever stop learning.

Be different. Think different. Be you. It's more fun, and your business will be the better for it.

Book & Resource Guide

Books

Business Plans for Dummies, Paul Tiffany & Steven Peterson, 1997, Hungry Minds, Cleveland.

Get a Financial Life, Beth Kobliner, 1996, Fireside Publishing, New York.

Growing A Business, Paul Hawken, 1987, Simon & Schuster, New York, New York.

Honest Business, A Superior Strategy for Starting and Managing Your Own Business, Michael Phillips & Salli Rasberry, 1981, Random House, New York.

How to Read a Financial Report, John A. Tracy, 1983, John Wiley & Sons, New York.

The Interpretation of Financial Statements, Ben Graham, 1937, Harper & Row, New York.

Natural Capitalism, Paul Hawken et al., 1999, Little, Brown & Co., Boston.

The Resume Handbook, Arthur D. Rosenberg.

Resume Writing, A Comprehensive How-to-do-it Guide, Burdette E. Bostwick

The Seven Laws of Money, Michael Phillips, 1974, Random House, New York.

Small Time Operator: How to Start Your Own Business, Keep Your Books, Pay Your Taxes and Stay out of Trouble, Bernard B. Kamoroff, 2002, C.P.A., Bell Springs Publishing, Willits, California.

Starting your Own Business, Jan Norman, 1999, Upstart Publishing, Chicago.

The Tao of Pooh, Benjamin Hoff, 1982, Dutton, New York.

Your Money or Your Life, Joe Dominguez & Vicki Robin, 1992, Penguin Books, New York.

Who Moved My Cheese, Spencer Johnson, M.D., 1998, G.P. Putnam & Sons, New York.

Book & Resource Guide

Internet Resourses
(Web Sites)

www.amazon.com -   search engine for books

www.budgetregister.com -   for registering your domain name

www.CarWizard.com   -   for buying autos

www.directnic.com   -   for registering your domain name

www.edmunds.com   -   for buying autos

www.ftb.ca.gov   - California Tax Board site, for state tax forms

www.forrestyoga.com - Forrest Yoga Web site

www.heathertiddensyoga.com - Heather Tiddens Web site

www.google.com   -   search engine. Look here for anything, & everything

www.imagroup.com -   check this for malpractice insurance

www.intuit.com   -   homepage for Quicken accounting and tax programs

www.irs.gov -   government income tax site

www.LeaseWizard.com   -   for leasing autos

www.microsoft.com   -   software of course

www.mindbodysoftware.com - software for studio management

www.sba.gov/indes.html - the Web site for the Small Business Administration; agency with government help for small businesses including loans.

www.score.com - service corps of retired executives has retired business people who volunteer their time; look for a chapter in your area.

www.server101.com - Web page hostings

www.ss.ca.gov/business - California State, business site, questions, forms, etc.

www.verio.com - Web page hosting site

www.theWellworks.com - software for studio management

www.yogatimes.com - useful trade magazine

www.yogajournal.com - useful trade magazine